Endorsements
10 Steps to Career Success
By Kathleen Brady

Get a Job, 10 Steps to Career Success will clarify the process of your career search. Anyone who is starting out, reinventing, or advancing their career must read this book. To neglect Kathleen's insightful recommendations, will put you at a professional disadvantage. Moreover, I recommend this book to all of my students.

Richard W. Stanton, MBA
Georgian Court University
School of Business

Kathleen Brady's wealth of experience advising job seekers at different stages of a career comes through loud and clear in her practical, step-by-step guide to finding a job that feeds both the body and the soul. The useful exercises and conversational writing style will get anyone paralyzed by the words Get a Job motivated and on their way to finding meaningful work.

Gihan Fernando
Executive Director, American University Career Center

Kathleen Brady again shows why she is one of the leading experts in her field. Her straight forward no nonsense approach to job seeking is absolutely necessary in today's workplace. She takes you through the process step by step and gives you the confidence and skills needed to succeed. A must read for job seekers........

W. Piercy
Job Seeker

Kathleen Brady's latest edition of *Get a Job!* will not only help you do that, but it will also help you get a Life, and I mean that in a good way! She gives readers excellent exercises in this workbook-like advice book. You will learn not just how to get a job, network and all things career-related, but you will also figure out your life rules, assess your values, and a lot more. Her insights are incredibly wise, from differentiating what we think we're supposed to do to her assessment that managing our career can be learned, just like driving a car. If you want to be happy in life and work, this is the book for you!

Russ Terry
Author of My Gratitude Journal & Founder/CEO of Life Coach Radio
Networks

Get a Job! is a very timely resource, since companies are more selective about hiring people than ever before. Kathleen Brady's *10 Steps to Career Success* fills in the gap where career and outplacement services don't teach. Brady breaks the fascination of Black-Hole submissions and provides a powerful alternative that must be embraced by all students and professionals.

Rod Colón
Rod Colón Consulting, LLC
Motivational Speaker, Master Networker, Career Strategist, Radio Show
Host, Corporate Trainer and Author

GET A JOB!

10 STEPS TO CAREER SUCCESS

By Kathleen Brady

Published by Motivational Press, Inc.
7777 N Wickham Rd, # 12-247
Melbourne, FL 32940
www.MotivationalPress.com

Manufactured in the United States of America.

ISBN: 978-1-62865-157-7

CONTENTS

INTRODUCTION

DEAR JOB HUNTER,

GET A JOB! These three powerful words often leave people paralyzed. Whether you are a recent graduate looking for your first job or a seasoned professional looking for a new job, the process can be daunting.

While there are many books and resources available to assist you with specific aspects of job hunting (like self- assessment, writing resumes, interviewing, and negotiating offers), **GET A JOB!** provides a comprehensive game plan that shows *how* all these pieces work in tandem. It offers practical instructions to show you exactly *how* to conduct meaningful self-assessment and *how* to craft a winning resume and cover letters. It describes *how* to network, *how* to interview effectively, and *how* to negotiate and evaluate offers. In the second edition, I added additional advice about career management (goal setting, communication, leadership and time and stress management), and provided details on proven workplace strategies to show you *how* to excel in your career. The advice is specific, but it is generic enough to be applicable across industry lines and experience levels.

As a career/life coach, it is clear to me that the skills and processes needed to build a successful career (goal setting, communication, leadership and time and stress management) are the exact same skills and processes needed to build a successful life. **GET A JOB!** shows readers how to integrate best practices "career advice" into their personal lives and how to infuse inspiring "life purpose" advice into their careers.

My vision is for you to use this publication as you would a travel guide. Much like a travel guide, you will want to skim through **GET A JOB!** to get a lay of the land. Next, you'll want to zero in on the chapter related to where you are on the job search continuum. As you work through the various exercises and activities, the book will direct you to other areas that will be helpful to you as you work your way through the process. I have left ample space for you to make lists, take notes, and highlight information. The book is designed so that you can jump around to reference the information that you need at any given moment.

Keep in mind, there is no "one size fits all" approach to job hunting and career management. The world of work is evolving every day. Worry less about doing it "right" and focus more on how your actions impact the image you are trying to project and the life you hope to live. Review these best practices, add your own wisdom and creativity, and be fearless in your approach.

GET A JOB! 10 STEPS TO CAREER SUCCESS is the travel guide for the most important journey of your life. Refer to it repeatedly throughout your career. Add notes and build on lessons learned and successes achieved. But most of all, enjoy the ride.

Wishing you great success,
Kathleen Brady

CHAPTER ONE

MEET YOUR FUTURE SELF: INTRODUCTION TO CAREER/LIFE PLANNING

External pressures to be "successful" in our careers compel us to approach life with a narrow focus. We make career decisions with little regard to the unintended consequences that they will have on the overall quality of our lives. We ignore the reality that our career and personal lives are integrally intertwined; choices made in one area greatly impact the other. Yet, most of us spend more time planning a weekend road trip than we do planning our careers, let alone our lives.

If you think about it, everyone is chasing a similar dream: to live a fulfilling, happy life, complete with meaningful work and supportive, loving relationships. Yet, when asked, most people struggle to articulate how they arrive at decisions that allow them to live their version of a "fulfilling and happy" life. In fact, most people cannot even describe what they mean by "fulfilling and happy." My purpose in writing this book was to challenge readers to not only define their vision, but to examine the unconscious, yet defining principals governing *how* they live their lives in order to make conscious choices that will lead to prosperity and joy. By exploring both the "what" and the "how" of career/life success, you will be able to answer the question, *"what do I want my life to look like?"* and then design a tactical plan to achieve that vision, balancing the competing priorities of your personal and professional goals.

Aligning your personal vision with the expectations and demands of the workplace is the often overlooked, yet critical element of career/life success. Too many people become trapped on a misguided path leading towards an unfulfilling career, and ultimately an unfulfilling life, because they make career decisions based not only on erroneous expectations about the workplace, but also based on what they think they are *supposed* to do instead of what excites and inspires them. Yet, by learning how to align the wants, needs, and values of the workplace with our individual wants, needs, and values, we can revolutionize how we work and live, to the benefit of employers and employees alike.

Let us start by considering the impact that your work will have on your life. Every job choice that you make will impact the quality of your career, which in turn will affect your entire life. These choices will impact your long term earning potential, your social circle, where you will live, if and who you will marry... everything. Therefore, the sooner you decide what you want long term and what you are prepared to sacrifice short term, the happier you will be. Whether you are 25, 45 or 65, whether you are looking for your first job or a career change, the rest of your life starts right now.

The skills and processes needed to build a successful career are the exact same skills and processes needed to build a successful life. These include self-assessment, goal setting, time management, communication, wellness planning, etc. There are a plethora of books addressing these areas as they relate to careers. There are also an equal number of books offering advice on how to live your best life, underscoring the same skills and processes, albeit with slightly different labels: self-reflection, identifying wants and needs, work/life balance, communication, stress reduction. **GET A JOB!** offers readers the best of both worlds by demonstrating how to integrate best practices "career advice" into your personal life and how to infuse inspiring "life purpose" advice into your career. It is designed to satisfy logical and emotional thinkers alike by exploring both the "what" and the "how" of success.

The good news is that despite current economic conditions there *are* jobs to be had at *every* level, as well as opportunities for advancement. Do not automatically accept the conventional wisdom that tells you that "you do not have enough experience" or that "you are overqualified," etc. Instead, develop the skills and insights needed to master the job search. It does not matter if you are looking for your first job or a mid-career change; the job search process is exactly the same. The people who are going to be successful at landing their dream jobs and advancing their careers are the people who:

- believe they can;
- know how to conduct an effective job search, and;
- are willing to put in the time and effort to make it happen.

Reading **GET A JOB!** and completing the exercises and challenges throughout the book will enable you to be one of those successful people.

Planning your career is like learning to drive a car. No one is born knowing how to drive or how to manage their careers – yet, both are very learnable skills. It is simply a matter of learning the rules.

Knowing that most people spend more time planning a weekend road trip than they do planning their career or life, think about the last trip that you planned. You likely chose a destination based on specific criteria about how you enjoy spending your time, and selected the best route to get there. Before you started your trip, you probably made sure your vehicle was operating at optimal performance and gassed up the tank. Perhaps you bought maps or invested in a GPS system, stocked a cooler with bottled water and snacks, and made sure your jumper cables were in the trunk, just in case of an emergency. You packed your suitcase with everything that you would need for your time away to ensure a safe and pleasant journey.

Why not apply the same process towards mapping out a career/life strategy? Think about what you like to do (what is the dream?), then research where the best place to do it might be. Gather the tools you need (skills, education, etc.,), plan for possible emergencies (like industry shifts, layoffs, and bully bosses) and you will have a safe and pleasant journey.

Some of you may be thinking, *"I haven't got time to be thinking about this stuff,"* because you either need to find a job or are busy doing your job. But, unless you pause to consider your options and map out your strategy, the choices you make today may take you in a direction that you do not want to go.

Too many people choose the path of least resistance and end up living an unfulfilled life. As a career coach, I have seen it countless times. For example, a finance major encountering a competitive job market opts to accept Uncle Lou's offer to work construction at his company. A perfectly fine job for someone who wants to do construction, but limiting for a person interested in working on Wall Street. Short term, the money may be good. However, long term, this job does not take that finance major any closer to the ultimate goal of working on Wall Street.

Similarly, some people avoid facing a tough job market by enrolling in graduate school, believing the added credential will ensure success. However, unless graduate school fits into your predetermined career plans, hiding out in graduate school until the economy improves simply exchanges one set of problems for another. While it allows you to avoid any timing gap on your resume, it also forces you to incur additional debt. Graduate school could add upwards of $100,000 to your debt burden, which would seriously limit your career options. An unpaid internship in your field or industry of interest, which allows you to expand your network and develop industry knowledge or volunteer work at any not-for-profit organization to build your skill set, may be a better option. They provide you with opportunities to gain valuable experience and meet people who could be helpful to you without incurring any additional debt.

Any action that takes you towards a goal that you are not interested in achieving is not worth taking. It is better to put your energy into finding a job that you actually want. However, and this is huge, that does *not* mean you can hide out indefinitely playing Xbox or watching reruns of Law & Order until the job market improves. It also does not mean that you must resign yourself to stay stuck in an unfulfilling job. You *must* take action towards achieving your goals every day. That is why it is so important to first *define* your goals. (You will have an opportunity to do that at the end of this chapter.).

You have the power to create the career — and the life — you want. It is simply a matter of deciding *what* you want and then *choosing* to invest the necessary time, energy, and resources to move you in that direction. You *can* accomplish everything you want and you *can* find your dream job and achieve life//work balance, providing you are willing to do what it takes to achieve your objectives.

Once you can identify *what* you want, next ask yourself "*why* do I want it?" The answer to why is actually the goal. Then, you must consider what you need to *do*, what actions you need to *take,* or what *choices* you need to make to get those things. Discerning the answers to those questions take time and reflection. (Chapter 3 offers tools to help you articulate your responses.) So many of us get caught up in things that keep us busy, but do not contribute to our life's happiness; we confuse activity with accomplishment. We do not pay attention to the choices we are making that may hinder our success.

Think about success for a minute. What does it look like? Odds are that every person reading this has a different answer. However, there are four common elements in every vision of success. They are:

1. Being content about your life;

2. Achieving measurable accomplishments that compare favorably to others with similar goals;

3. Believing that you have a positive impact on people you care about most;

4. And, leaving a legacy.

Each element contributes to the way you experience success *right now*. Success is *not* merely a future event or something to aspire towards. Think of it also as a current state of being: the ability to pay full and undivided attention to what matters most in your life at any given moment. Of course, deciding "what matters most" may not be as easy as it sounds. (Chapter 3 will help clarify that for you.)

We know that our work and personal lives are integrally intertwined; the days of working 9 to 5 and living 5 to 9 are long over. Choices we make in one area greatly impact the other, but still, we are not particularly clear about what is most important to us. We arrive at decisions on the basis of short-term focused, money-power-status type motivations without any thought.

External definitions of success seem to take precedent over our internal rubrics when we are faced with an important career or life choice. Perhaps because they are louder, we assume these external rules are our own. We accept societal pressures dictating which career path to follow, where to live, whom to marry, what type of car to drive, etc., with little thought to the impact these decisions will have on the overall quality of our lives. We accept these guidelines because, without introspection, they are the only ones that we hear. As a result, the day to day choices we make are governed by "should" thinking. If you are feeling stressed, overwhelmed, or disconnected, it is likely because those external rules are in conflict with your yet-to-be-examined internal rules.

Your internal life rules are the principles and standards by which you make decisions – both big and small – that impact the quality of your life. They are shaped by your values, faith, and belief systems. Unless forced to do so by some external life event, people rarely spend much time thinking about such things. The death of a loved one, graduation, loss of a job, marriage, divorce, and parenthood are examples of major life moments which compel us to pause and reflect on the things that are most important to us. It is during those moments that we ask ourselves the hard questions:

What am I doing?
Why am I doing this?
What is the purpose?

However, as soon the event passes, we return to our daily lives without fully considering the answers to those significant questions. We dismiss such reflections as self-indulgent, navel-gazing silliness, instigated by a momentary ordeal. There are bills to pay, chores to complete, family responsibilities to tend to, work pressures to overcome, bucket lists to fill, etc. We remain unaware of *why* we make the choices we make and resume the activities that keep us busy, yet not necessarily happy or fulfilled.

Consider what your career/life might look like if you took the time to think about *what* you are doing and *why* you are doing it in order to live your life consciously.

Everything that you do requires a choice. There are the big choices: where to live, what career path to follow, who to share your life with, your faith, etc. Then, there are the small choices: what time to wake up each morning; what to eat, what to wear, how to spend the day, how to respond to people and events. The small choices seem inconsequential. Some people would argue that they are not really choices at all, but rather decisions dictated by life's external pressures or requirements.

But they are choices.

You choose to get up at 6 a.m. to catch the 7:09 train to get to work despite the fact that you would rather sleep until noon because you know that the price that you would have to pay to sleep until noon is too high. If your goal truly is to sleep until noon each day, you would choose a different job and lifestyle to accommodate that goal. The seemingly small choices you make daily ultimately determine the quality of your life.

Such "self-indulgent navel-gazing" will ultimately spare you pain and misery because you will be able to identify and eliminate useless activities and needless stress. You will be able to answer the hard questions and define the purpose of your career/life choices. Armed with an understanding of your life rules, you will no longer feel compelled to accept a job because you believe you "should" but rather will have the confidence to select one that will bring you joy. When we acknowledge and honor our values, faith, and belief systems we are able to eliminate the fear that drives us to stay stuck in unfulfilling jobs and partake in non-productive, frenetic activities. Suddenly, the meaningless busyness and annoying stresses of daily life are replaced with a calming sense of acceptance of the world around us.

Before you fling this book across the room in disgust at wasting money on yet another self-help book filled with platitudes preaching the virtues of positive thinking, let me assure you nothing is further from the truth. Positive thinking without action amounts to magical thinking, which is a complete waste of time. People sometimes confuse bumper stickers and clichés with their life rules. Slogans like *"Just do it," "Go for it!" "Don't Sweat the Small Stuff!"* and *"Be fearless!"* may serve as marvelous mantras and offer momentary inspiration, but do they really drive the way you live your life? How often do you "just do it" or "go for it"? Do you truly not "sweat the small stuff"? Are you "fearless"? To dig deeper than clichés, examine your actions.

This book is designed to help you find that sweet spot between the land of rainbows and unicorns (where everything is possible) and reality (where the obstacles are real). You will discover how to embrace your personal and professional dreams – to imagine what is possible - and learn how to make conscious choices about which actions to take to **GET A JOB!** and design the career and life that you envision for yourself.

CHALLENGE: What are Your Life Rules?

Your life rules are the deeply held, sometimes unconscious belief systems that govern your actions. As an example, I share the following 7 rules that serve as my guiding principles for how I want to live my life.

- Be kind to others (and myself).
- Be honest and direct – even when it is uncomfortable.
- Remember there are 3 sides to every story/situation.
- Always go for the laugh.
- If you don't ask, you don't get.
- Live simply.
- Trust God.

No matter what is going on around me, I can call on one of these rules to guide me. They allow me to show up in every situation the way I want to show up; that is to be the person I want to be. I consciously choose behaviors to honor these rules.

Like most rules, it is easy to be tempted to break them. It can be extremely hard to be kind to people who are behaving meanly. Oftentimes. it would be much easier to avoid an uncomfortable conversation with a friend or colleague than it is to be honest and direct. Yet, I have learned, when I break one of my rules, I experience a greater discomfort. It means that I have allowed an external person or event to control my behavior; I have relinquished control and responsibility.

Articulating and honoring your life rules will allow your inner and outer selves to be as one, and at peace. It is in achieving that peace that we are able to experience life with greater clarity.

These rules work for me; they are not designed to work for anyone else. I challenge you to articulate the life rules that work for you. How do you want to show up at work, at home, in life? I have no doubt you have been living them. The next step is to live them consciously. What are YOUR life Rules?

What are YOUR Life Rules?

Keep in mind, living consciously does not eliminate the stresses, challenges, and sorrows of life; it simply offers the strength to cope with whatever comes your way. It works because, as the Law of Attraction reminds us, we attract our dominant thoughts. If you believe that you will encounter insurmountable obstacles at every turn in life, you will. If you believe there is a solution to every obstacle, you will see the solution. That does not mean the obstacle does not exist nor does it mean that the solution is easy. It simply means your efforts will not be thwarted; you will make a conscious choice to manage whatever is getting in the way of your success.

There will always be a price to pay for the choices you make. Whether you recognize it or not, you are paying a price right now for the unconscious choices that you are making. Living consciously at least allows you to negotiate the price up front.

People often think they *could* achieve their dreams *if only* they had more time, money, or luck. While all of those variables may influence the outcome of any objective, none of those things will ensure success. Think of all the examples of people who succeed without them. So, if it is not time, money or luck, what is the secret?

The secret to success is *energy*. Energy is your most valuable resource; it is not time, not money, not luck. Energy is the fuel needed to realize your dreams. It is created by a sense of purpose and living a life that integrates your needs, wants, and gifts. If you are feeling overwhelmed, depressed, exhausted, burned out, or defeated, your energy level will understandably be low. The same is true if you are feeling angry, fearful, anxious, defensive, or resentful. Your energy is not productive, and you end up spinning your wheels.

"If only" people construct a reality out of the world around them where success and happiness is impossible because they focus on the *obstacles* that exist to thwart their efforts rather than the *choices* available to overcome or manage them. They are paralyzed by fear of the unknown or they fixate on problems and assigning blame. They tell themselves, *"I can't because..."* They blame their boss, spouse, lack of money, or the weather for their inability to achieve their goals. They cannot see the choices available to them to overcome the obstacles.

"What if" people, on the other hand, focus on solutions to problems. They assume responsibility for future outcomes and take control of their fate. They are able to identify the choices they have and design a course of action to achieve their goals (or modify them when necessary). Their faith in their own abilities is undeniable. They simply *believe* they can and that belief provides them with the productive energy that they need to take action.

CHALLENGE:
I can't ....

List all the things you would LIKE to do, but believe you are not capable of doing.

CHALLENGE:
HOW can I?

For each item listed, brainstorm possible answers to the question HOW can I?

Managing your career or life requires a comprehensive plan, updated annually, outlining goals and objectives designed to be flexible enough to accommodate unexpected changes. Without a plan, your career or life will suffer. To create your plan, identify at least 25 things that you want to accomplish during your lifetime. Think about what you want to *have*, what you want to *be*, what you want to *do,* and what *impact* you want to have. Consider all areas of your life career: financial, social cultural, spiritual, family home, education, health and fitness. Write down your goals. Written goals give your dreams structure. They create a long-term perspective and enable you to prioritize so that you can manage conflicting goals and deal with unexpected transitions. Once you see everything on paper, you can begin to prioritize your goals in the context of your current life situation.

Studies suggest that during your twenties and early thirties, you are likely to:

- Commit to an occupation, lifestyle, spouse;
- Focus on "establishing" yourself within your chosen profession;
- And, concentrate on your career "advancement," with a vision toward the future. Typically, the career trajectory during this phase is a steep incline with well-defined benchmarks to assess growth.

Sometime during your late thirties and early forties, you may:

- Discover your choices are no longer rewarding;
- Experience a "period of crisis" as the result of some life-altering event (death of a parent, birth of a child, divorce, etc.);
- Become more specific about your needs, focusing on the here and now;
- Reassess your choices;
- And, accept your current situation or opt for change.

The trajectory during this stage is less steep, and in some instances, even flat. At this stage, you have proven what you can do and now you are deciding if you *still want* to do it. For some, this period provides an opportunity to reap the benefits of years of hard work; they allow their careers to operate on automatic pilot while they tend to other facets of their life. For others, it is a time of discontentment and frustration as they try to determine what lies ahead.

By the time they reach their late forties and early fifties, most people are old enough to have acquired considerable life experience and to have learned from it, yet are young enough to act on it and make the necessary course corrections by readjusting goals and shifting priorities. People may opt to change careers, change lifestyles, or both.

They may also opt to do nothing. Recognize that opting to do nothing is a choice, too.

Whichever stage you are at, ask yourself, *what do I really want to do*? Not what makes sense or what your spouse, parents, or friends want you to do, but what do *you* really want to do? Allow yourself to dream at this stage. Dreams foster hope and open our minds to the possibilities. Do not allow limiting beliefs, previous disappointments, criticisms, or failures to stifle your dreams. Ask yourself: *"what might I attempt if I knew I could not fail?"*

If your goals do not move you, if they do not inspire and incite you to action, they are not the right goals. Too many people try to alter themselves to suit their "should" goals. That is a bit like wearing the wrong size shoe because it goes with your outfit. It can work for a short time, but eventually, it becomes uncomfortable and ultimately unbearable. Therefore, do not "should" all over yourself.

The right goals outweigh any excuses you have to achieve them. It won't matter if you don't have any experience or have too much experience or went to the "wrong" school, or selected a "useless" major, or are male or female, black or white, gay or straight. Your passion and commitment to your goal will fuel your efforts.

Do not underestimate the power of passion. The world is filled with examples of people who achieved their goals — against all odds — because of their passion. Consider Neil Parry, the San Jose State football player whose right leg was amputated below the knee after a horrific injury in a game during the 2000 season. Hours after his leg was removed, Parry vowed he would play football again, an unlikely proposition under the circumstances. Yet, in September 2003, Parry was back on the field and fans were hard pressed to notice a difference between his abilities and those of his two-legged teammates. It was not easy, but he had the drive and passion to withstand 25 operations and countless hours of rehabilitation and physical therapy to achieve his goal. If you allow yourself to be fueled by your internal drive instead of any external pressures, your shortcomings will have little or no impact on your ability to succeed. They may present hurdles, but your passion will galvanize your abilities, skills, strengths, and talents so you can easily clear the bar.

Exercise 1: Identify Your Career /Life Goals

1. List the important things you want to accomplish during your lifetime. Do not worry about whether or not these things are practical, or even possible, just yet. Allow yourself to dream. When you are satisfied with your list, date it. These are your **lifetime goals.**

2. From that **lifetime** list, select the four or five things you want to accomplish in the next five years to create your **5-year plan.**

3. Review your 5-year plan and choose the two or three things you want to accomplish during the coming year. These are your **annual goals**.

4. For each **annual goal** listed, write down the answer to the following questions.

- *What* is the goal?
- *Why* do I want to achieve this goal?
- *When* will I achieve this goal?
- *How* will I achieve this goal? (Or: *What 3 things do I need to DO?*)
- *Who* can help me achieve this goal?

Repeat this process once a year, referring back to your *lifetime goals* and *5-year plan*. Revise each list as circumstances warrant.

Once you are clear about what you want and have an action plan in place to guide you, you will see just how possible impossible really is. By following the steps outlined in this book, you will be well on your way to securing the job—and ultimately the career and life--you want. To get yourself started, decide how much time and effort that you are willing to devote to this process. Maintaining a steady and consistent effort will be one of the most important elements in determining your success. Accept that there will be peaks and valleys in the process. There will be days with a great deal of activity and positive feedback, and there will be days when you feel like you will never find a job or advance in your career. Those are the days that it is important to find a way to reenergize and motivate yourself. Spend time with friends and family, tackle a long overdue project, or volunteer your services; do whatever you need to do to remind yourself of your gifts, talents, and competencies. And remember, this is a temporary situation.

Because each job choice and career decision you make throughout your professional life is likely to have an enormous impact on your personal life, getting started can be scary and overwhelming. Do it anyway. I promise that the rewards will be worthwhile.

CHAPTER TWO

STEP 1: LEARN THE JOB SEARCH PROCESS

Typically, job seekers start their search in the middle of the process instead of at the beginning. They start by drafting a resume, simply listing all their experiences in reverse chronological order. But a resume needs to be more than just a laundry list of your education, employers, and job titles. A resume is a sales document; it is your marketing brochure. To ensure that you design an effective one, you have to know what you have to sell *and* you have to understand who your target audience is. That is why the chapter on resumes comes in the middle of the book (Chapter 4) and not at the beginning.

Job hunting and career management are not linear processes; they typically are not even logical processes. Career/life planning in general, and job hunting in particular, involve three phases that sometimes move in a circuitous motion; these are oftentimes overlapping with each other.

Phase 1: Know Yourself

During this phase, the focus is inwards. At every stage of your career you not only have to know, but you must be able to articulate the *value* you have to offer employers. You must continuously invest time to:

- Identify your values, skills, and abilities;
- Recognize your technical knowledge;
- Evaluate your experiences;
- List your accomplishments;
- Acknowledge your educational level;
- Recognize your preferred work styles;
- Consider your temperament;
- Examine your interests;
- Understand your motivations;
- And, set goals.

Phase 2: Assess Your Market

The focus during this phase is outwards. Knowing what *value* you have to offer, you now must learn how employers view the abilities, skills and talents you identified in Phase 1. During this phase you must:

- Review job postings;
- Research individuals, organizations, and communities;
- Talk to business associates, friends, and family members;
- Read trade papers, blogs, and websites;
- Develop contact lists;
- And, conduct informational interviews.

This step is not just for job seekers. Even if you have a job, you must do these things too, albeit at a more relaxed pace. Think of it as a "passive job search." While you may not be looking for a new job, the information you uncover will provide the opportunity to continually reassess the value that you have to offer your current employer, and ensure you remain up-to-date and relevant in your role. You will uncover any additional skills or core competencies you need to develop to advance in your career.

Phase 3: Take Action

It is only after you understand what you have to offer, and who needs what you have to offer, that you can focus on the mechanics of job hunting and career management. Now, it is time for job seekers to:

- Draft resumes, cover letters, and applications (revise as needed);
- Interview for positions;
- Negotiate salaries;
- And, evaluate offers.
- and for employees to:
- Add to your technical skill set and knowledge base;
- And, develop the requisite core competencies in the "silent discriminator" soft skills like leadership, teamwork, communication and time/stress management.

But remember, the process is not as linear as these steps suggest. It is circular and continuous. For example, information discovered during market assessment may require you to revisit Phase One and revise your goals or rework your resume. An unsuccessful interview in Phase 3 may point you back to Phase 2 to do more in-depth market research. Every step along the way is meant to teach you something about yourself or about the world of work. It can be overwhelming and disorienting, like being lost on a road trip, but you may just discover a path you had not even considered. Be open to the journey.

Here is how to put the winning career/life management formula (Self-Assessment + Market- Assessment = Career Success) into action.

Phase 1: Self-Assessment *Action*

Dare to Dream

Follow your passion! Do what you love! Look for your dream job!
These pearls of wisdom have become part of the daily lexicon

for job seekers, instilling fear and anxiety for the very people they are meant to inspire. Some worry that they are not *passionate* about anything; others lament the impracticality of pursuing the *dream job*. There are mortgages and tuitions to pay and Johnny needs braces; there are student loans and car payments and dreams of moving out of childhood homes. Given today's economic climate, they say, *dream jobs* can only be found in the world of unicorns and rainbows. The very words meant to encourage and incite job seekers have instead stymied them.

Some of the synonyms for the word "passion" include, "desire," "urge," "ache," and "fervor." Let us be realistic: most of us do not "ache" for our jobs, no matter how much we enjoy them. What we are really passionate about is that our job is aligned with our *values*. Perhaps, instead of trying to identify your passion, ask yourself what values you hold and consider how your job or career reflects those *values*. What is *important* to you?

Exercise 2: What are *Your* Values?

Using the following scales, each value on a scale of 1 to 5 based on its IMPORTANCE in your life and on how well your current career/life choices honor each value.

1 Extremely Important 2 Very Important 3 Important 4 Not Very Important 5 Not At All Important

1 Extremely Fulfilled 2 Very Fulfilled 3 Fulfilled 4 Not Very Fulfilled 5 Not At All Fulfilled

	Importance Rating	Fulfillment Rating
Achievement		
Advancement		
Adventure		
Aesthetics		

	Importance Rating	Fulfillment Rating
Affiliation		
Altruism		
Authority & Power		
Autonomy		
Being Needed		
Challenge		
Change		
Clarity		
Closure		
Commitment to Goal(s)		
Communication		
Competition		
Competence		
Connecting to Others		
Complexity		
Control		
Courage		
Creativity		
Direct Impact		
Discovering New Things		
Diversity		
Economic Return		
Education		
Effectiveness		
Emotional Growth		
Excellence		
Excitement and Adventure		

	Importance Rating	Fulfillment Rating
Fairness		
Family		
Flexibility		
Focus		
Freedom		
Fringe Benefits		
Friends		
Fulfillment		
Fun		
Harmony		
Health or Physical Fitness		
High Profile		
High Risk or High Reward		
Holistic Approach		
Honesty		
Humor		
Improving the World		
Independence		
Individuality		
Influencing People		
Innovation		
Integrity		
Intellectual Stimulation		
Interesting Work		
Intimacy		
Job Security		
Joy		

	Importance Rating	Fulfillment Rating
Justice		
Knowledge		
Leadership of Others		
Leisure Time		
Lifestyle Integration		
Location		
Loyalty		
Mentoring		
Morality		
Nature		
Nurturing		
Openness		
Orderliness		
Partnership		
Personal Growth		
Physical Appearance		
Physical Challenge		
Physical Environment		
Pleasure		
Popularity		
Power		
Privacy		
Professionalism		
Recognition		
Relationships		
Religious Observance		
Respect		

	Importance Rating	Fulfillment Rating
Responsibility		
Romance		
Routine		
Salary		
Security		
Service		
Social Relevance		
Specialization		
Spirituality		
Stability		
Status		
Structured Environment		
Supervision		
Supervision of Others		
Training		
Traveling		
Trust		
Truth		
Upward Mobility		
Variety		
Vitality		
Working Alone		
Working on Teams		
Other		

"Look for your dream job" isn't bad advice, however, the dream must be tempered with reality. The trick is to examine your "reality" to discover how real it actually is. Typically, when you feel tied financially to your work but disconnected emotionally, there is a sense of being trapped. You cannot see the alternatives. You only see the obstacles and that kills the dream prematurely. However, you must spend time in the dream to consider how to convert *"I can't because..."* thinking into *"how can I..."* thinking in order to see past the obstacles. (Review the Challenge from Chapter 1.) It is very possible that your original interpretation of "reality" was incorrect.

At the other end of the spectrum is the person holding out for the dream job, refusing to enter the workforce until the opportunity is "perfect." That person believes in the unicorns and rainbows. How real is *that* reality? It is important to recognize that the dream job is not likely to be the first stop on the career train; but, you have to get *on* the train. The key is to make sure that you get on a train going in the direction that you want to go. If a career in finance is what you are seeking, working in your Uncle's construction company is not going to get you there unless it is paying the bills while you get your MBA. The reality is, there are sacrifices and adjustments that need to be made while pursing the dream. It *is* possible to balance the dream with reality, but you have to be willing to give equal attention to both.

Ask yourself: *what is my dream job?* Don't worry, *for the moment,* if the job makes does not make sense, or if you are overqualified, underqualified, too young, too old, etc. Do not worry about pay scales or additional training needed. For the moment, just think about what you would like to *do*. Once you identify the dream, the practicalities will come into play to shape the direction of your job search. The trick is to not let those practicalities stifle the dream prematurely. There may be ancillary careers that can put you in the arena of your dream job.

For example, let us suppose the dream job is to be a pitcher for the

New York Yankees. Rather than simply dismiss that as an impractical dream, brainstorm what other positions might be available that incorporate a passion for baseball with your current skill set. Are there positions at organizations such as Major League Baseball, Tops Baseball Cards, Spalding, Nike, the players' union, etc.? Which firms or companies work with or for the owners, players, or specific teams? Have any of the players established youth baseball camps, restaurants, or clothing lines? What role could you play in those ventures? Think creatively. Think big. Once you have a general direction, it will be easier to strategize how to get there.

Some people are unclear as to what the dream is. Allow yourself to be playful at this stage. Think back to your response the first time an adult asked you "w*hat do you want to be when you grow up?*" Rather than dismiss your childhood dream to be a pirate, consider *why* you wanted to be a pirate. What was appealing about that career path? Was it the clothing? Perhaps you would enjoy a career in fashion design. Was it the fact that pirates do not have to shower? Brainstorm career paths where being dirty is acceptable. Maybe, it is the sense of adventure and being on the open seas that you found appealing. How about a career in the Navy or as a marine biologist, or as an environmental engineer?

I purposefully picked a silly example to demonstrate how useful dreams can be towards helping you establish real goals and move forward. Embrace the dream; explore its meaning.

As you work through this book, you will note the exercises and challenges are designed to be thought-provoking. They may make you uncomfortable because the answers are not readily available to you. That is ok. Think of the discomfort as part of personal and professional growth leading to greater clarity and ultimately the ability to live and work more joyfully.

Exercise 3: Reflect

As part of the self-assessment process, consider your responses to the following questions. Consider the choices that you made. Jot down your responses. Note any patterns, themes and inconsistencies. These are not easy questions. Take time to truly think about them.

- How do you **describe your current job or career** to others?

- At the **start of your career**, what were your ambitions or long term goals?

- Thinking about your **first job**, why did you make that choice? What were you looking for and how did it advance or contribute to the achievement of your ambitions or long term goals?

- Consider your **first job change**. How did it come about? Who initiated the change? What were the reasons for the change? How did you feel about it? What impact did the change have on your ambitions or long term goals? (Repeat this question for each additional job change.)

- Reflecting upon your career to date, can you identify times when change seemed more than routine? What **life event(s)** served as the catalyst(s) for change? How did you feel about it? What impact did the change(s) have on your ambitions/ long range goals?

- Are there periods of your career or life that stand out as particularly **happy or enjoyable times**? What made them enjoyable?

- Are there periods in your career/life that stand out as particularly **unhappy or difficult times**? What made them unhappy or difficult?

- What **messages** did you receive about work during your formative years?

- What did your **parents or significant adults in your life do for a living**? What were their views towards work?

- What did your **parents or significant adults in your life want you to do** for a living?

- What do your **siblings do** for a living? What are their views towards work?

- If you **are struggling** to make a career or life decision, can you describe **why**?

- **Have your goals changed** since you started your career? When? Why?

- How do you see your **career or life progressing** over the next decade?

- BONUS QUESTION: **Why** do you work?

Chapter three will offer you further opportunities for self-assessment to define your abilities, skills, and technical expertise. For now, the objective is to help you to think about the dream. If you still are struggling to articulate the "dream job," the following Challenge may be helpful.

CHALLENGE

Imagine it is one year from today, and you have *the perfect job* and are living your life exactly how you want to be living it. Write a brief paragraph addressing the answers to the following questions.

What are you doing?

(Incorporate as many aspects of your life as possible)

(What does your morning routine look like? What are you wearing to work? What is your commute like? What does your work environment look like? With whom are you doing it? What tasks are you performing? What is your interaction with co-workers/clients/bosses look like? What time are you leaving? Do you take work home with you? What role does technology play? Where are you living? How much income are you earning? How much fun are you having? What impact are you making on the world each day? What do your senses pick up? How do you feel?)

Phase 2: Market Assessment Action

Market assessment enables you to understand, and ultimately articulate, the value you have to offer employers. The Internet makes it easy to conduct market research. Review job descriptions on job boards like Indeed or CareerBuilder. You could also google *"jobs for math majors"* or *"jobs in sports marketing"* to find niche websites. To learn about job outlooks or position requirements, check out http://www.bls.gov/ooh/occupation-finder.htm. Finally, see the appendix for a list of useful websites.

Exercise 4: Conduct Market Research

Review a variety of job postings and notice your reaction to them. Do they sound interesting and exciting? Is it something that you think that you would enjoy doing? If so, print those out and put them in a folder. Again, at this stage, do not worry about being overqualified, underqualified, too young, too old, or about pay scales or additional training. Remember, you are still exploring the dream. Do this over the course of a couple of days, or even weeks. Once you have 20 or 30 postings, review them and consider what they have in common. For example, do they all involve working with people or data; are they all various roles within a particular industry; are they concentrated in a specific geographic location; do they all require a specific skill or talent? Pay attention to the words that are used to describe the position. (These will be important later when you are crafting your resume and cover letters.) A career coach or other objective person can help you see what they have in common if you cannot see it clearly. With two or three directions to pursue, you can investigate further.

There is a wealth of information beyond simple job listings that can assist you in keeping abreast of marketplace trends and understanding how to highlight the abilities and skills you have — or need to acquire – to ensure employability. There are databases containing information about industry trends, specific company profiles, relocation information, salary levels, etc. With over 40,000 employment related sites in existence, you are sure to find the preliminary information that you need. But it can be overwhelming. With so many resources and so many different things you can do on the web, it is hard to know where to begin.

Start with a trip to your local public library. There, you will find valuable, easy-to-use resources and services – including the expertise of librarians – to add power to your job search, at no additional cost to you. Libraries offer a plethora of services, including free computers to conduct your job search and classes on a variety of job search related topics. They have subscriptions to various newspapers and periodicals that can save you hundreds of dollars. They offer guidebooks, videos, and electronic books for self-instruction. While you can certainly access some of these things at your local Unemployment Center, the library offers more convenient hours, a nicer ambiance, and – no disrespect to the dedicated staff at unemployment centers – a highly trained team of skilled professionals to assist you.

It is access to the premium databases — worth *thousands* of dollars that make the trip to the library imperative. Perhaps the greatest challenge for job seekers face is finding the *name* of someone inside a company to contact. **Reference USA Business Directories Online** solves that dilemma. It is a suite of directories of all U.S. employers, including government and non-profit entities. Job seekers can tailor searches by industry, size, and location and get detailed information about the company, including contact names of people in management (which you can then cross reference on LinkedIn. We will talk more about LinkedIn later.) Best of all, you can create and download your very own contact list of potential targets. **EBSCO Business Source** and **EBSCO Regional Business News** are great resources to find information on smaller, regional employers.

All you need is your library card – your tax dollars at work.

Exercise 5: Bookmark Useful Websites

Identify 10 – 12 sites that are most likely to serve you best (see appendix). To help you assess which are the best ones to use, consider:

- The number and kinds of jobs posted on the site;
- The primary salary levels of the posted jobs;
- The cost of using the site;
- And, the availability of other job search information, such as interview preparation, negotiating tips, etc.

You also want to make sure the site is well-maintained, regularly updated and easy to navigate.

Consider using electronic "job agents" and joining "talent communities" on specific company websites. These are functions offered by some websites that allow you to enter your employment objectives and automatically notified you whenever there is a match. As powerful and convenient as they are, job agents should not be a substitute for the host of other activities that you must be involved in to conduct an effective job search; they are one of many resources available to you. Remember, you are *not* ready to apply to any positions just yet. At this stage, you are looking to uncover information.

Because you need to be prepared to have the salary conversation whenever the employer brings it up, before you meet with anyone, consider how much money you need to earn in order to maintain your current life style. Write out a detailed budget for yourself and your family. This preliminary investigation into salary will help you later on as you negotiate opportunities.

Exercise 6: Review Your Budget

It is important to do the math and know what your monthly cash outflow is. Multiply by 12 months to come up with a *target net* annual salary needed. Keep in mind that the stated *gross* salary is the amount of money that your employer pays you. The *net* pay is the amount of money that you receive after deductions. Aim for a *gross* salary that is approximately one third more than your net needs. Be sure to include:

Mortgage/Rent _____

Gas & Electric _____

Telephone _____

Cable/Internet _____

Loans (Student, Personal and Home Equity) _____

Car Payment _____

Car Expenses (gas, parking, tolls maintenance) _____

Insurance (Health, Homeowners, Disability, Life) _____

Medical Expenses _____

Dental Expenses _____

Public Transportation _____

Personal Care (haircuts, etc.) _____

Groceries _____

Savings _____

Professional Membership Fees _____

Charitable Contributions _____

Child Care _____

Tuition _____

Pets and Pet Care _____

Health Club or Gym Fees _____

Clothes (Laundry and Dry Cleaning) _____

Entertainment _____

Magazines, Newspapers, and Books _____

Home Expenses _____

Gifts _____

If your monthly net need is 6000 multiplied by 12, you need a net salary of $72,000 plus $24,000 (1/3 of $72,000; a rough estimate to cover taxes) for a gross salary of $96,000.

It is important to recognize that what you *need* is not necessarily what employers will think that you are *worth*. While the seller may set the price, it is ultimately the buyer who determines the *value*. Review annual salary surveys published by trade magazines and associations to get a ballpark figure of the going rates. Keep in mind that these numbers are not absolute figures; they should be used to help you calculate an appropriate salary range for positions based on a realistic assessment of what the market will command. This information will be critical during the negotiating phase of a job search campaign. Check out www.payscale.com and www.salary.com for the most current information. Also, google *"salaries in XYZ industry."*

Finally, you must understand what you can expect from the internet. Sitting home in your pajamas applying to jobs online is not likely to yield the results you want. Studies indicate that approximately 4-6% of new hires come from job boards. The percentage is higher for company websites, but it is still under 25%. If you dedicate 90% of your time to an effort with such a low rate of return, you will be missing opportunities. While the internet is a great tool at this research stage, you must use it in conjunction with every other resource available to you in order to be effective.

Phase 3: Take Action - *Action*

Chapters seven through nine outline job search mechanics in greater detail, offering best practices related to how to draft resumes and cover letters, prepare for interviews, negotiate and assess offers, and build core competences to sustain advancement. But you must spend time doing self-assessment and market research first in order to articulate your storyline and create effective materials to get the job in the first place.

A job hunt does not have to be a devastating experience; it does not take guts so much as it requires thought, persistence, and a willingness to make choices to achieve a long term goal. Keep in mind that job searches take time, effort, and creativity. It is not necessarily the most qualified person who gets the job; rather, it is the person most skilled at finding a job. Focus on the *process.*

Allocate a Specific Amount of Time

To get yourself started, you must decide how much time that you can realistically devote to your search. If you are currently working, or are a full time student, consider between two and three hours per week; if you are unemployed, consider five and seven hours per day. Maintaining a *steady and consistent* effort throughout your search will be one of the most important elements in determining your success. A "start and stop" approach almost always leads you back to square one at each juncture. Working in bursts of activity will ensure failure. Sending out a stack of resumes six months ago does not entitle you to say *"I've been looking for 6 months"* if you have done nothing to follow up.

Adhere to a Schedule

Regardless of how many hours you have allocated to the process, work out a schedule and make a personal commitment to stick to it. During those reserved hours, your job search must be your primary focus. This is the time committed to self-assessment exercises, making phone calls, conducting research, etc. Do not allow yourself to be interrupted by running errands, baby sitting, etc. By adhering to a schedule, you will reduce the insecurity most job seekers feel because you will be in control. You will also be able to chart your progress.

Select a System to Record Your Activities

Whether you opt for a notebook and pen, an elaborate computer based system or an app, you must develop a system for recording your activities in order to easily retrieve important data and to ensure appropriate follow-up actions. Be sure to include:

- Target Employer (name, address, phone, email);
- Primary Contact;
- Date Contacted;
- Follow-up Action (five to seven days after initial contact);
- End results;
- And, additional info (i.e., source of lead).

Use All Available Resources

In addition to your public library and the unemployment centers, consider returning to your college campus to schedule an individual appointment with a counselor at your school's Office of Career Services. An initial appointment with a career counselor (generally free of charge) can provide information about the type of services that your school offers its students and alumni. For example, nearly every school has as intranet job board containing job listings of positions. These offer a wealth of information and possible job leads because many schools receive listings from their alumni that are not published elsewhere.

Also, look for industry associations that offer job search assistance for a specific target audience. Google *"Job search resources for lawyers/dancers/veterans/mechanics/etc."*

Finally, consider engaging an independent career or executive coach. The initial investment is likely to save you thousands of dollars in the long run, as well as hours of time and aggravation running in circles.

Tend to Your Emotional Well Being

Your emotional well-being deserves attention and care throughout the process. In fact, your productivity and ultimate success depend on it. This is the hardest part for most people. A job search creates a tremendous sense of anxiety. The things that people typically fear most about a job search include:

- Financial considerations;
- Self-doubt;
- Loss of status/identity;
- Disruption of familiar and comfortable routines;
- Fear of the unknown;
- And, not getting along with new co-workers or supervisors.

Analyze the panic. How real are these fears? How can you prepare for, minimize, or render any of these scenarios temporarily? Share your anxieties with friends or family. Not only can these people be great sounding boards, but they can also help you spot flaws in your approach. However, if you believe a well-meaning spouse or parents will drive you crazy by trying to be helpful or asking too many questions or by simply nagging, politely ask them to leave you alone while you sort through things. Consider hiring a career coach who can offer objective feedback and insights.

Keep in mind a change in your life naturally means a change in the life of your family members. They may be scared, or have questions as well. Do not try to protect loved ones by acting as if you are in control. They will be more supportive if they know what is going on and understand how they can be helpful.

Because the very nature of the job search process invites rejection, it is important to design strategies to work through the rejection so that you have the energy to move on to the next call, meeting, or interview, which may be the one where you land the perfect job. So, how do you tap into your productive energy? It is simple: change your mindset.

Whatever the task may be that is depleting your energy level, keep in mind that it has no inherent emotional value. It is how you describe it that suggests your reaction to it and ultimately the amount of energy you will be able to muster up to complete it. Our brain assigns every event, experience, and situation a "label." Those labels are determined by our *NAIL filters,* which ultimately impact our energy levels.

Negative Talk: - The first nail is that little voice inside you that tells you *"you can't because"* you are not worthy of achieving your dream. *You aren't good enough, smart enough, thin enough, etc.* When we listen to that voice, we are usually focused on fear, not possibility. Challenge that voice. What makes you think you are not enough? How true is that belief?

Assumptions: Sometimes we hold onto an expectation that because something has happened before it will happen again. How true is that belief? How can you behave differently to influence the outcome?

Interpretations: We sometimes form opinions or judgments and believe them to be true without any investigation. Why not test your hypothesis by asking a question. Perhaps there is an alternate way to view the situation.

Limiting Beliefs: These are the things you accept about life, about yourself, or about the world that hold you back. (*Employers don't hire anyone over 50; you cannot get a job without experience; it is an old boys club, etc.*) Again the question is, how true is that? What is another way to look at that?

Everyone struggles with their NAILs to varying degrees. The trick to tapping into your productive energy is to become aware of which of these things is interfering with your success. The next time you feel stuck, challenge your own thinking and ask yourself: *What is another way to look at this?* Even if you do not wholeheartedly agree with the other possibilities, just knowing there *are* alternate perspectives will help to loosen the grip of those NAILs and allow you to change the label, evoke a new feeling, and take a different action. *You can* shift your energy level. You simply have to believe it is possible.

Finally, in order to maintain a sustained, consistent effort, break the job search process down in to small, manageable steps. If you wake up each morning and declare, *"today, I will find a new job,"* you are setting yourself up for failure; you will become overwhelmed and subsequently paralyzed. Ask yourself instead, *"what can I do today?"* and then do it.

Allow yourself time to be with the important people in your life who can provide support, encouragement, and perhaps a few laughs during this challenging time. Do not feel guilty about enjoying something or goofing off periodically. Exercise, take a short trip, tackle a project, or read a novel. A short time away from your job search may allow you to return with renewed vigor and energy.

Exercise 7: Develop Your Weekly Action Plan

Create a Weekly Action Sheet to establish short term goals and monitor your progress. Be sure to include:

- The specific number of hours you can commit to your job search;
- The tasks you will *accomplish;*
- The things you must *do* to accomplish these tasks;
- Possible *obstacles* and *challenges* to prevent you from accomplishing the tasks;
- And, strategies to *overcome* obstacles and challenges.

Finding the courage to forge your own path and construct a personal definition of success in the face of external obligations and pressures is not easy. Focus on the action steps, trust the process, and you will arrive at your destination.

CHAPTER THREE

STEP 2: CRAFT YOUR MESSAGE

By now, you realize that self-knowledge gained through self-assessment exercises like those found in chapter two is the most reliable tool you can use to run an effective job search and ensure career success. It is your job to know what you have to offer in order to meet the needs of your target employers.

Employers selected candidates based on *their* needs, not yours. Therefore, job seekers must be able to demonstrate exactly how they can meet employers' needs. They must be able to articulate their skills and abilities, temperament, and preferred work style, passions and values, motivations and goals, and accomplishments and knowledge base in order to interview successfully and land not just *a* job, but the *right* job. To do this, you must understand the ABCs of job hunting:

Abilities (catalogue your talents, skills, accomplishments and special knowledge);

Beliefs (acknowledge your motivations, passions, values, goals, and ideals);

Communication (consider your temperament, work style, and communication patterns).

In tough economic times, job seekers dismiss the importance of self-assessment, viewing it as a luxury that must be sacrificed to obtain a job. Instead, they allow the market to dictate career and job choices. That is the exact wrong way to approach your job search. It is *especially* critical in a tumultuous job market to focus on self-assessment. Your challenge is to explain how what you can do and what you know is of value to the employer. Jobs are joint ventures in problem solving. The idea is to find a match between an employer's needs and your abilities and skills. Therefore, you need to have a keen understanding of how you process information, solve problems, make decisions, and communicate.

Two basic questions apply to every career (and thus every career plan): (1) what needs to be done (uncovered through market assessment), and (2) what can *you* do?

Let us start by identifying what you can do.

Exercise 8: Discover Your Abilities and Skills

Qualities needed for Success

I have the ability to:

Accept responsibilities	1 2 3 4 5
Adhere to deadlines	1 2 3 4 5
Adapt to change	1 2 3 4 5
Apply legal or business principles	1 2 3 4 5
Analyze data	1 2 3 4 5
Assemble deals	1 2 3 4 5
Assimilate new data quickly	1 2 3 4 5
Be self-directed	1 2 3 4 5
Be responsive, reliable and conscientious	1 2 3 4 5

Build internal/external networks	1	2	3	4	5
Collaborate with colleagues	1	2	3	4	5
Communicate orally	1	2	3	4	5
Communicate in writing	1	2	3	4	5
Compete	1	2	3	4	5
Conceptualize	1	2	3	4	5
Conduct research	1	2	3	4	5
Confront people	1	2	3	4	5
Counsel or advise clients	1	2	3	4	5
Decide in pressure situations	1	2	3	4	5
Delegate	1	2	3	4	5
Demonstrate commitment	1	2	3	4	5
Demonstrate good judgment/common sense	1	2	3	4	5
Demonstrate political judgment	1	2	3	4	5
Develop business	1	2	3	4	5
Develop rapport and trust	1	2	3	4	5
Digest large quantities of material	1	2	3	4	5
Draft documents	1	2	3	4	5
Editing	1	2	3	4	5
Empathize	1	2	3	4	5
Explain complicated ideas in simple terms	1	2	3	4	5
Facilitate	1	2	3	4	5
Follow through	1	2	3	4	5
Formulate strategy	1	2	3	4	5
Gather facts	1	2	3	4	5
Initiate	1	2	3	4	5
Inspire confidence	1	2	3	4	5

Interview	1	2	3	4	5
Keep confidences	1	2	3	4	5
Lead	1	2	3	4	5
Listen critically	1	2	3	4	5
Manage complex tasks	1	2	3	4	5
Manage people	1	2	3	4	5
Mediate	1	2	3	4	5
Motivate	1	2	3	4	5
Negotiate	1	2	3	4	5
Organize	1	2	3	4	5
Persuade, promote, or sell	1	2	3	4	5
Predict or forecast trends	1	2	3	4	5
Prioritize	1	2	3	4	5
Produce quality work	1	2	3	4	5
Put in long hours	1	2	3	4	5
"Read" people	1	2	3	4	5
Research	1	2	3	4	5
Resolve Conflicts	1	2	3	4	5
Retain information	1	2	3	4	5
Schedule deadlines, set goals, and maintain 'systems'	1	2	3	4	5
Solve problems creatively	1	2	3	4	5
Speak persuasively	1	2	3	4	5
Summarize	1	2	3	4	5
Supervise	1	2	3	4	5
Synthesis	1	2	3	4	5
Take risks	1	2	3	4	5
Theorize	1	2	3	4	5

Tolerate delays, wait	1 2 3 4 5
Train/Teach	1 2 3 4 5
Troubleshoot	1 2 3 4 5
Understand objectives, practices and work standards	1 2 3 4 5
Use technology proficiently	1 2 3 4 5
Work well under pressure	1 2 3 4 5
Work efficiently	1 2 3 4 5
Write persuasively (reports, memos, proposals)	1 2 3 4 5
Write technically	1 2 3 4 5

Step 2: For those characteristics that you ranked low, consider whether you need to develop this skill further to meet market challenges. If so, design a strategy to address it. For example, if you have not had the opportunity to manage others and ranked yourself low, consider setting a goal to take a management course in the coming year.

For each characteristic you ranked 5, go back and add the phrase "for example," and offer proof. Examples are the best way to showcase your strengths and highlight your contributions and value. You will be able to use these stories to demonstrate to an interviewer that you are the ideal candidate for a job.

Example: I have the ability to organize. For example, I organized a job fair coordinating 200 employers, and 900 students from 14 different schools. My job was to make sure that every student was in the proper place every 20 minutes and that the employers had the correct resumes.

Identify Your *Success* Patterns

Transferable/functional abilities are ways that we characteristically react to problematic situations throughout life. As a child, if confronted with a puzzle or task, your reaction may have been to organize the pieces and then examine alternative solutions. As a teenager repairing a car engine, the same problem solving abilities may have been utilized. These problem-solving patterns are known as "success patterns" and tend to become set during the teenage years. Over the years, we tend to become more proficient in the use of our favorite abilities, but because they seem innate, we do not always recognize them as marketable skills.

To help you identify your success patterns and marketable skills, think about what you have already achieved or accomplished. Include things related to work, leisure, and education. An accomplishment can be something big like planning a fundraising event, winning a jury verdict, or landing a big client. Or, it can be something very simple, like receiving an A on a school project, hosting a surprise birthday party for a friend, or managing a personal crisis. Your ability or skill patterns will emerge no matter which accomplishments you select. Divide your life into segments to ensure that you cover the entire spectrum of your life (i.e., "High School, College, Graduate School, Job #1" or "Teens, 20s, 30s, 40s" etc.) Review files, look through yearbooks, and family photo albums to help jog your memory. You may not be able to complete this exercise in one sitting. Consider doing it over the course of a few days, adding accomplishments as they occur to you.

Exercise 9: Catalogue Your Achievements

Step 1: Define the segments of your life and then list a total of 10 accomplishments, with representation from each segment.

Life Segment A	Life Segment B	Life Segment C	Life Segment D
Accomplishments:	Accomplishments:	Accomplishments:	Accomplishments:

Step 2: Select three or four accomplishments on your list that you would like to examine more closely. Describe the accomplishment while answering the following questions:

- What was the subject matter?
- What was the environment like?
- What abilities or skills did you use? What did you do best?
- What did you enjoy most?
- What was your key motivator?
- What was your relationship to others?
- Concentrate on *how* you did it, but do not analyze.

Have fun with this – do not worry about grammar, spelling or punctuation. At the end, note how you felt at the conclusion of the event.

Samples

1: In the fourth grade, every student had to do a presentation on a specific country. I was assigned Guatemala. Determined to get an A, I went to Funk & Wagnall's encyclopedia to do my research on the population, climate, etc. I also went to the library and took out all the books that I could find on that country to ensure I knew all there was to know about Guatemala. I copied information onto index cards and organized the cards into categories. Unlike my classmates, I was excited about standing in front of my classmates and showing off how much I knew. My teacher told me that I did a good job and gave me an A+. I felt proud.

2: In senior year of college, I took an elective course that required an oral presentation at the end of the semester. Because the course was in my major, I was well versed in the subject matter and not overly concerned about the presentation. The day before the presentation, I spent about 15 minutes organizing my thoughts. The following day in class, another student asked if she could deliver her presentation first because she was very nervous and wanted to "get it over with." She had handouts and diagrams, and despite how prepared she was, she appeared flustered and unorganized. When it was my turn, I walked to the front of the classroom with my half page of notes feeling slightly worried that I did not have all the supporting documentation she had. But I delivered my presentation— barely referring to my notes—in an interesting and engaging way. The audience applauded and I received an A. (They didn't applaud for my classmate and she only got a B.) I remember feeling surprised at how easy it was and feeling slightly superior to my classmate who had clearly invested more time in preparing than I had.

3: I am extremely proud of having my nonfiction book published. I spent several months researching the topic, drafting the chapters, and putting the information together in a way that I believed would be useful to the reader. A friend of a friend presented the draft to a small, independent publisher who agreed to publish it. In order to boost sales, I scheduled several presentations on local TV and radio shows, Barnes & Noble bookstores, etc. The publisher printed twice as many copies as he expected and told me how pleased that he was to find an author who wrote well and who enjoyed the marketing component of the book business.

From the sample stories, one might assume that the author enjoys being recognized as an expert and has an innate ability as a public speaker. The author demonstrated research and writing abilities, as well as oral presentation talents. This information is important to know and easy to translate to employers during the interview process. *("Ever since the fourth grade, I knew that I enjoyed researching topics and was comfortable speaking in public. Those skills will serve me well as a trial lawyer.")*

Step 3: Your Stories: Review your stories, circling all skills mentioned. Read the stories aloud to a friend or colleague, and ask them to note the skills they heard. (This is a great way to learn how you are perceived by others.) Note any themes and patterns.

In addition to knowing what you can do, choosing the right career path also requires insight into your personality. Understanding your temperament will enable you to select an environment compatible with your preferred work style.

For example, introverts and extroverts thrive in different work environments. Introverts are often quiet and reflective. They like to have time to process information before articulating their thoughts. They like a more stable, consistent work environment. Extroverts get their energy through external events and other people, so they generally like a faster paced environment. They tend to think "out loud" and enjoy plenty of interaction as well as variety in their tasks. An extrovert forced to sit at a computer alone all day would be unhappy (and ultimately unsuccessful) just as an introvert forced to interact with others all day would be unhappy. Of course, some people fall in the middle of the introvert-extrovert scale and find they need a workplace that provides a combination of such activities.

Knowing where you fall on this scale will enable you to consider what types of bosses, colleagues, clients, and subordinates that you work well with, and in what environment you are likely to feel most comfortable.

You also need to understand which of the following you prefer:

- Dealing with facts and data or people and emotions;
- Solving problems in a linear, logical manner or holistically;
- Making decisions intuitively or deductively;
- And, working in a structured or unstructured environment.

There are a variety of self-assessment tools that are designed to help increase your understanding of yourself. While no one test is going to provide you with all the answers to guarantee career success, any one of the assessments described in this chapter, in conjunction with a trained career coach, can provide useful insights to help you design a focused but flexible career plan.

The Highlands Ability Battery (www.highlandsco.com) is a tool that offers insight into your temperament, as well as your natural abilities. While the words "abilities" and "skills" are used interchangeable throughout this book, there is an important distinction to be made. A true ability is demonstrated when a particular task comes easily, quickly, and effortlessly; it is the way a person is "hard- wired." Skills, on the other hand, are learned through training, practice, and experience. Knowing your natural abilities can help steer you toward tasks and roles that use your best talents and steer you away from tasks that would be difficult and unfulfilling for you to learn. Many smart people acquire and employ skills that play against their natural abilities and become quite successful in doing so. Yet, they are never completely satisfied. Similarly, if you do not have an opportunity to use your natural abilities in your job, you may become frustrated in your work.

Based on the work of research scientist Johnson O'Connor, this online assessment tool uses 19 different timed work samples to measure the speed with which a person is able to perform a particular series of tasks. The scores, shown together on a personal profile and bar chart, reveal patterns or "clusters" of abilities that highlight your natural gifts and talents in relationship to how you learn, how you solve problems, how you communicate, and even which type of work environment best suits you. A certified provider offers a skilled analysis of the written report and helps individuals explore the best career options based on their natural abilities.

Strengths finder is another excellent resource. This book by Tom Rath provides a code to take an assessment online that measures the presence of 34 talent themes. It offers insights into your top five themes, describing your naturally recurring patterns of thought, feeling, behavior, and the impact on your behavior and performance.

The online **Self-Directed Search** (SDS) (www.self-directed-search.com) provides an individualized interpretive report describing what you like — your favorite activities and interests — as well as information about potentially satisfying occupations. The SDS was developed by Dr. John Holland, whose theory of careers is the basis for most of the career inventories used today. According to Dr. Holland's theory, people are most satisfied in their careers when they are surrounded by people with similar interests because it creates a work environment that suits their personalities. People are more comfortable, and ultimately more successful, in a work environment that rewards the traits and behaviors that come most naturally to them. Holland's theory states that most people can be loosely categorized with respect to six types:

- **Realistic:** likes to work with things more than with people;

- **Investigative**: likes to explore and understand things or events rather than persuade others or sell them things;

- **Artistic:** likes creating original work and has a good imagination;

- **Social**: likes to be around people, is interested in how people get along, and likes to help people with their problems;

- **Enterprising**: likes to persuade or direct others more than work on scientific or complicated topics;

- **Conventional**: likes to follow orderly routines and meet clear standards, avoiding work that does not have clear directions.

Occupations and work environments can also be classified by the same categories. The interpretive report provides a list of career options that match your results and offers direction about where to focus your market research.

Another assessment to consider is **The Myers-Briggs Type Indicator (MBTI)**. It is based on the theory that individuals are either born with, or develop, certain *preferred* ways of thinking and acting. By examining your responses to a series of questions, the MBTI defines 16 possible psychological types. These combinations indicate your preferences for the following:

- **E**xtroversion and **I**ntroversion: whether you get energy from being around people or from time spent alone;

- **S**ensing and i**N**tuition: whether you enjoy working with facts and concrete details or prefer to focus on hunches and the big picture;

- **T**hinking and **F**eeling: whether you tend to make decisions based on logic and the principles involved or on your values and promoting harmony for the people involved;

- **J**udging and **P**erceiving: whether you prefer your life to be planned and decided, or prefer to go with the flow and like keeping your options open.

This test is offered online (www.mbticomplete.com) without the assistance of a qualified counselor or can be administered through a qualified MBTI career counselor who will help interpret the results.

Finally, the **DiSC Sort** is offered online (www.disctests.com) and classifies four aspects of behavior by testing a person's preferences in word associations. DiSC is an acronym for the terms below:

- **Dominance**: People who score high in the intensity of the D styles are very active in dealing with problems and challenges, while those with low D scores want to do more research before committing to a decision.

- **Influence**: People with high I styles scores influence others through talking and activity and tend to be emotional. Those with low I scores influence more through data and facts, not feelings.

- **Steadiness**: People with high S styles scores want a steady pace, security, and do not like sudden change. Low S intensity scores are those who like change and variety.

- **Conscientiousness**: People with high C styles scores adhere to rules, regulations, and structure. They like to do quality work and do it right the first time. Those with low C scores challenge the rules, want independence, and are uninhibited by details.

Both MBTI and DiSC provide an individualized written report. While you do not need a certified career counselor to interpret the results, someone trained in interpreting these tools would be extremely useful in terms of guiding you toward the practical application of the information on designing your career plan. Check with the career development office of your college or graduate school to see if anyone on staff is certified in these instruments. They are typically willing to meet with alumni on a limited basis.

This is just a sampling of assessment tools available. In my opinion, they are the best on the market. Understand that you *do not* need to take all of them. Pick one, maybe two, to help you gain additional insights into yourself and help you clarify your goals.

It is important to consider the competencies and personal qualities that you want to live by and see reflected in the workplace. Value your unique gifts and talents and you will, in turn, be valued by others. Catalogue your skills, abilities, and special knowledge continually, and be prepared to tell people about them. Do not think of it as shameless self-promotion; instead think of it as sharing relevant information with people who can help you achieve your goals.

Exercise 10: Draft Your Preliminary Marketing Statement

Having mastered the ABCs of the job search, you are now ready to draft your preliminary marketing statement. Write out exactly how you want to present yourself. Be sure to include:

- The type of position you are seeking;
- The geographic areas you are considering;
- The special knowledge, abilities and skills you have to offer;
- And, your short and long term goals.

Once you have the basic information assembled, massage the sentence structure and syntax until you create a 10-15 second self-introduction that sounds natural and rolls easily off your tongue.

Your Marketing Statement

CHAPTER FOUR

STEP 3: DESIGN YOUR MARKETING MATERIALS – RESUMES, COVER LETTERS, AND ONLINE PROFILES

Goals have been written; self-assessment has begun and research is underway. it is time to focus on your marketing material. Every self-marketing kit should contain a resume, LinkedIn profile, cover letter, and references. Some industries may also requiring transcripts, writing samples, portfolios, or other ancillary documentation relevant to your applications.

Let us start with the resume. Think of it as a sales document. To design an effective sales document, you must have a clear idea of the job that you are seeking so that you can skew your resume to your target audience. An effective resume provides not only a clear understanding of what you have done but, more importantly, how that experience is relevant to the potential employers. That is why we have spent so much time concentrating on self-assessment and preliminary market research. (We will cover market research to a great extent in chapters five and six.) Ideally, you created a resume file early in your career, adding experiences and accomplishments as they occurred. You should update this document throughout your career. But, even if you have not created one, now is as good a time as any to begin. First, decide which information to include; pay close attention to the words that you use to describe your experiences. Many employers use computer algorithms to scan resumes, searching for specific words or phrases. You want to use industry specific jargon to describe your experience. Then, concentrate on the format and style that you want to use to best display your content.

Your resume is an opportunity to create a positive impression with an employer. Because this document is a self-portrait, it is difficult to give generic advice on the preparation of a resume. There are no absolute rules to follow. Anyone who gives you resume advice that starts with *"you should always"* or you *"should never"* is wrong. Your resume is as individual as you are. There are many good websites that offer industry specific samples that you will want to review to get some ideas (Google "sample resumes for *insert job title*"). Check out the website www.bestsampleresume.com for some industry-specific ideas.

While there are no absolute rules, there are key concepts and general rules of thumb to follow concerning format and content no matter what industry you are interested in.

- **A resume should be brief.** Conventional wisdom suggests resumes should be one page long. However, if you have had an extensive career, you do yourself a disservice by eliminating relevant information or cramming your content into one page. Expand to a second page. Make sure the second page is at least half full, with your name, address, telephone number, and e-mail at the top.

- **Simple, descriptive language is key.** Typically, computers read your resume first and software is designed to search for specific words, so format your electronic resume to work for you by investing the time to tailor it to specific positions. Try to incorporate the language used in the job postings to describe your experiences.

- **Name, address, phone number, and e-mail should appear at the top of the resume.** Phone numbers are essential and your voicemail message should be clear, professional and preferably in your voice. Also, be sure to have a professional e-mail address. Partygirl@gmail.com does not suggest a professional persona.

- **A *Job Objective* is not necessary.** Your objective is to get the job for which you are applying. An objective focuses on what you want, not what you have to offer. Instead, consider a *Career Summary,* which highlights your professional background as it relates to the position that you are seeking. It should consist of several statements that demonstrate your abilities, skills, and credentials. Describe what you can do, not what you want to do. Avoid the overuse of adjectives. You can modify this section as needed to appeal to specific employers without needing to revamp your entire resume to pierce through computer screening systems.

- **The *Experience* section can be formatted either chronologically or functionally**. Chronological resumes are oriented by date, with the most recent position first and proceeding backward. This is the most popularly used and accepted format because it is logical and easy to follow. This is the format to use if you have a steady work history with no gaps and if your most recent job is related to your job target. If you have a substantial work history, consider adding Accomplishments under each entry to focus the reader on your successes. If you are switching directions, a functional resume may be more effective. Here accomplishments and experience are organized under broad areas of expertise or skills headings with the most important category (to the potential employer) at the top, followed by two or three other functions. This format allows you to organize your experience according to your talents. It also allows you to de-emphasize employment dates, company names, and titles, which should be included under the heading *Employment*. Check out www.bestsampleresume.com for free examples of resumes in a variety of industries.

- **The *Education* section should contain all pertinent information from your college or graduate school experience**, including the official name of the schools, years of graduation, and a list of any appropriate academic and/or extracurricular activities. If you have attended an Ivy League school, consider leading with the *Education* section. If you had stellar grades in school, you may also want to keep your education section first for your first year or two after graduation. Otherwise, your education should go after experience.

- **Consider including a section that draws attention to unique skills such as foreign languages or personal interests.** The section may be titled *Personal* or *Interests.* Its purpose is to facilitate conversation or "break the ice" during an interview and to give the employer a more well-rounded appreciation of your background. Make sure that your personal interests are descriptive—e.g., "*travel to the Far East, Mexican cooking, and nineteenth century literature*" are much more effective than "*travel, reading and cooking.*"

- **Also consider adding a section for *Professional Affiliations* and/or *Community Activities.*** This will enable you to list church or synagogue activities, board memberships, volunteer work, and any other extra-curricular or leadership positions on your resume.

- **No personal information (height, weight, age, marital status, or health)** need appear on your resume.

- **Prepare a list of references** that is separate from your resume. Prepare a separate sheet of paper listing references (three is usually an adequate number) to have available when you go in for an interview. Include your references' affiliations, titles, and contact information. Ask people if they would be willing to serve as a reference *before* you give out their names and contact information. Even if someone has agreed in the past, it is important to check in with them again if some time has lapsed. The more your references understand about the job for which you are applying, the better able they will be to tailor their remarks in a favorable way. Be prepared to provide them with a copy of your resume and a "cheat sheet" that underscores the abilities, skills, and talents that you are highlighting to employers.

Other tips and techniques to keep in mind:

- Use strong action verbs to describe experience and accomplishments. Be specific.

- Use "bullets" if your descriptions are longer than 5 lines. Start each with an action verb.

- Use CAPITALIZATION, **bold print,** *italics,* underlining, indentation, and outline format to present information. Make it easy for the reader to scan. Research suggests that employers spend about six seconds with your resume before deciding whether to put it in the "yes" or "no" pile. Make sure the overall look is neat and clean.

- Use generous margins (but not so generous as to look skimpy). Balance the text on the page.

- Put dates on the right hand margin instead of the left so they do not stand out to the point that the employer will be distracted from the more important aspects of your resume.

- Proofread to eliminate errors and typos.

- Proofread it again!

Once you have created your resume, you need to ensure it translates properly via e-mail. Send it to a few friends to make sure it opens properly, and that there are no formatting issues. (For example, you may need to eliminate headers and/or footers.) When emailing your resume, it is best to send as a PDF file. You should also use the *Save As* function on your computer to create a second version of your resume in ASCII text or Rich Text Format. These are easier to use when posting resumes in online databases. (We will discuss this in greater detail in chapter six.) Proofread the new document to be sure information translated properly during the reformatting process. Finally, recognize that some employers, fearful of computer viruses, may not accept e-mails with attachments. In those instances, send your resume as the text of an e-mail message.

Exercise 11: Complete Resume Worksheets

Use this format to compile all the information for each category - include everything. You may ultimately decide not to include certain information on the resume, but do not edit at this stage. It may be worth including a college internship or long since past experience if it is relevant or uniquely interesting.

Education (Include the official names of the schools, years of graduation, and a list of any appropriate academic and/or extracurricular activities; if you are a current student with significant activities, list *activities* as a separate category.)

Experience (Include full time and part time positions. Compile the information chronologically. You can decide later how to format the information on the resume. You may include volunteer positions or leadership activities in this category *or* in separate categories.)

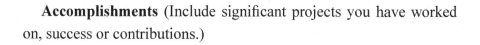

Accomplishments (Include significant projects you have worked on, success or contributions.)

Professional Affiliations (List Association Committees, Board Memberships, industry groups, etc.)

Community Activities (List pro bono activities, community groups, volunteer work, etc.)

Personal (List unique abilities, skills, or interests.)

For sample resumes in every industry, check out www. bestsampleresume.com.

Typically, when asked *"what do you do?"* people respond with a title. *"I'm a student/ doctor/ teacher/ lawyer/plumber, etc."* That rarely gives people enough information about you and it presents a unique challenge to job seekers who do not have a title. Instead, answer the question "what do you *do?*" by focusing on verbs. Be sure to use powerful language to describe your capabilities.

Exercise 12: Select Action Verbs to describe what you do

Consider the list of action verbs below. Highlight the verbs that best describe what you do. Be sure to incorporate them into your draft resume and in your self-marketing statement in chapter three.

Administrative: I....

accelerate	establish	prioritize
accomplish	examine	produce
arrange	execute	recommend
classify	file	record
collect	handle	reorganize
compile	led	review
compute	manage	schedule
coordinate	organize	streamline
delegate	overhaul	supervise
develop	oversee	word processing
direct	plan	

Communication (Oral): I...

address	convince	interpret
advocate	debate	interview
arbitrate	elicit	joke
argue	explain	judge
articulate	express	lecture
collaborate	influence	listen
consult	interact	mediate

moderate	present	solicit
observe	recruit	speak
participate	resolve	suggest

Communication (Written): I....

advertise	market	summarize
author	outline	synthesize
draft	persuade	translate
edit	present	write (technical)
explain	promote	write (speeches)
express	report	
influence	speech writing	

Creative: I...

act	establish	photograph
conceptualize	formulate	revitalize
create	illustrate	shape
compose	imagine	simplify
design	improvise	sing
develop	invent	stage
direct	model	visualize
entertain	perform	

Financial: I....

account	calculate	project
administer	forecast	purchase
allocate	formulate	quantify
audit	invest	rate
balance	monitor	record
budget	negotiate	report

research	simplify	translate
review	solve	uncover
save	theorize	value
scrutinize	track	

Human Relations: I...

adapt	educate	refer
advocate	empathize	rehabilitate
advise	encourage	represent
aid	ensure	rescue
answer	facilitate	resolve
arrange	guide	serve
assess	help	simplify
assist	intervene	supply
clarify	listen	support
coach	mentor	volunteer
collaborate	motivate	
counsel	prevent	

Management Leadership: I...

accomplish	consider	enhance
achieve	consolidate	generate
administer	control	hire
advise	coordinate	improve
analyze	counsel	increase
appoint	decide	institute
approve	delegate	lead
assign	direct	mentor
chair	emphasize	motivate
communicate	enforce	navigate

negotiate	plan	streamline
organize	preside	supervise
persuade	review	train

Problem Solving: I...

analyze	reason	present
decide	recognize	promote
diagnose	validate	represent
examine	conduct	research
execute	consult	respond
plan	inform	write
prove	plan	

Research: I....

analyze	extract	locate
assess	evaluate	measure
calculate	examine	organize
clarify	extrapolate	search
collect	formulate	solve
compare	gather	summarize
detect	inspect	survey
diagnose	interview	synthesize
explore	investigate	test

Selling: I....

build relationships	inform	present
communicate	organize	promote
contact	persuade	schedule
educate	plan	

Technical: I...

adjust	engineer	program
align	install	repair
assemble	observe	
draft	operate	

Teach/Train: I...

adapt	enable	instill
advise	encourage	instruct
clarify	evaluate	motivate
coach	explain	persuade
communicate	facilitate	plan
critique	focus	stimulate
develop	guide	teach
demonstrate	inform	

The purpose of your resume is to present your abilities, skills, and credentials in an appealing way that inspires the reader to want to meet you. Make sure that the overall appearance is attractive. It should be interesting and compelling, with a layout that looks professional and is visually appealing. Make sure you have emphasized your accomplishments. problem-solving abilities, and skills, and provided specific information about projects, products, and quantities with numbers or percentages whenever possible. Remember all sentences and paragraphs must start with strong action verbs in the present tense for your current job and past tense for all others.

Video resumes are just one of the new emerging technologies impacting job hunting. Some employers are beginning to accept them, but the trend has not quite caught on yet.

There are companies offering to produce professional video resumes. Before you invest in this, consider whether or not your target industry accepts them. If you opt to make one yourself, keep in mind things like lighting and background noise, along with powerful presentation skills, will all work in tandem to create a perception of you. Be sure to "test drive" your video resume with those in the workplace (not just fellow job seekers) before you submit it to employers. Ask them, *"would you hire the person in the video?"* Remember, you never get a second chance to make a first impression.

The same is true for social media. It also plays a role in how potential employers see you, so you want to consider your electronic reputation at the early stage of your job search. It is important that your profiles on various sites adequately convey the image that you want people to have of you.

Most people use Facebook to maintain social relationships, and LinkedIn to foster professional relationships, yet they are not exclusive. Potential employers look at both. Many job seekers have been disqualified based on sparse LinkedIn profiles or posts ranging from silly to inappropriate on Facebook. Claims of *"I'm not like that at work"* or *"I was just goofing around with some friends"* fall flat as your judgment is called into question. Every joke, tweet, or picture creates an impression of you that can never be undone. The good news is that you can control the impression. Be smart about it. Refer back to your "Life Rules" in chapter one, and make sure that you are walking the talk.

Your profiles and posts are similar to your resume in that they create an impression of you before people meet you. If you feel the need to share information about drinking, drug use, or your sexual escapades, use the setting options to limit who can see those posts. Any information shared publicly should be carefully considered, including the profile picture that you select. Make sure that it passes the "Grandma Test."

If you would not want your grandmother to see the post, it does not belong on the internet.

On LinkedIn, list interesting and relevant jobs, internships, or volunteer work. List the schools that you have attended, and any awards that you have won. The more complete and detailed your LinkedIn profile is, the more points of connection you will find. However, there is no need to list everything that you have ever done. Again, think about the image that you are trying to create. Seek recommendations from former employers, colleagues or clients to add strength to your profile. (Endorsements are different. Because they simply require clicking a button, they have become somewhat meaningless.) Finally, create a LinkedIn vanity URL to include on your resume. Simply click on your name in the upper right corner and select *Settings, Edit your Public Profile, Your Public Profile URL.* (We'll talk more about LinkedIn in chapter five.)

Post updates periodically about your activities to keep people up -to-date. Remember, this is the place to highlight a success or an expertise. It *is not* appropriate to post comments about any job search angst. Always maintain a business-like tone and consider what impression you are creating with your posts.

You are now ready to continue with more in-depth market assessment.

CHAPTER FIVE

STEP 4: NETWORK! NETWORK! NETWORK!

Armed with information about yourself, a draft resume, and your marketing pitch, as well as preliminary internet market research, it is now time to test the waters by talking to people: otherwise known as networking.

Countless books and articles have been written outlining networking techniques and gimmicks to coach readers. However, you *will not* be effective with empty techniques and gimmicks. Networking rests on the basic principle that businesses, jobs, and careers are built on personal relationships; therefore, *it must be genuine and sincere to be successful.*

Many people hate the thought of networking and are hesitant about "using" people or asking for help. Try to reframe how you think about it. Most people like to help others and those people in a position to help you might be insulted that they were not asked for assistance. It makes them feel good, powerful, and important. If you are doubtful, consider whether you would be willing to share your knowledge or give names to friends or business associates in order to be helpful. When you establish a specific and relevant basis for a conversation — to ask for ideas, opinions, a reaction to your own thoughts — there is no reason for you to be turned down. Ask for something specific, something that your contact can easily do.

The true purpose of networking is to get AIR: **a**dvice, **i**nformation and **r**eferrals. It occurs naturally in all areas of life. For example, when moving into a new neighborhood, you probably would not hesitate to ask your new neighbors for recommendations about dry cleaners, grocery stores, dentists, etc. Or, when planning a vacation you would not think twice about asking friends or family to recommend hotels and restaurants. In business, it is common to ask colleagues to suggest accountants, bankers, or computer systems. But, for some reason, we hesitate to ask people that we know about job opportunities. College friends, professors, family members, former employers, colleagues, neighbors, etc., are most likely in the best position to connect you to others in a position to hire you.

The first step is to identify *who* can help. Prepare a list of people with whom to network. Think about family members, friends, classmates, co-workers, professors, managers (past and present), service industry professionals (doctors, lawyers, accountants), or professionals in the field. Consider all the people you know: commuter buddies, your parents' friends, and people from your gym, school, or religious institution. Then, consider all the people that they know. Add to the list every day. Keep track of who referred you and how people are connected to each other.

LinkedIn is a great resource for that. Launched in 2003, LinkedIn is the largest and most powerful business focused social media network, linking over 135 million people. Anyone can sign up, and for free. Members can upgrade to a premium account, but the free service is all that the average job seeker needs.

LinkedIn is optimized to perform well in search engines, so it is easy to find people (*and be* found). Adding contacts is the driving force behind LinkedIn, but be selective about people that you connect to. Focus on quality, not quantity. Initially, limit it to people that you know well enough to phone or email. Send them a personalized email invitation to link. Generic invitations are cold and impersonal, and do little to foster the relationship. Eventually, you can add new people that you meet through your contacts, or at conferences and other professional events. *("I enjoyed hearing your presentation at the XYZ Conference last week. I'd like to add you to my network.")*

Next, decide *what* you want from each contact. You need to have a clear objective about what you are trying to accomplish before you contact anyone on your list. *Think through your strategy first.* Why have you selected this person to contact? What information do you hope to learn? To whom can they introduce you? There should be no mystery or hidden agenda as to the purpose of the conversation. Consider the following sample approaches to potential contacts:

- **To a geographic contact**: *"You have lived in this city for so long and know almost everyone..."*

- **To a socially active friend**: *"You have so many friends, you probably hear about things before anyone..."*

- **To someone who works in your field**: *"You have been working in the same type of job that I am looking for; I am sure you have some idea how my abilities and skills might be viewed..."*

- **To a professor**: *"You know better than anyone what kinds of jobs are open in this field..."*

- **To anyone that you admire**: *"You always seem to have good ideas..."*

- **To someone that you have helped**: *"We have helped each other in the past, so I am hoping you can help me now..."*

- **To a LinkedIn connection**: *"I saw that you are connected to Joe Smith at ABC corporation. I am interested to learn more about that organization. Could you introduce me?"*

It is important to understand what you can reasonably expect from professional relationships and what is outside those bounds. It is reasonable to expect:

- Information;
- Referrals to others who can help you;
- Reactions to your ideas and theories;
- Assistance in formulating plans;
- Feedback about resumes, cover letters and approach;
- And, moral support.

It is *not* reasonable to expect *a job* will be handed to you.

Most people do not know of many current job openings. If the first and only question posed to your contacts is *"do you know of any openings?"* you will more often than not receive a *no* and an opportunity may be lost. By asking questions like *"what do you do and what alternatives are out there?"* or *"where do you see someone with my abilities and skills fitting in?"* or *"do you know anyone who works at X?"* you will uncover information that will eventually generate opportunities, preserve your relationships, and enable you to reconnect with your contact throughout the job search process.

It is important not to limit your efforts to only those with influential positions and the power to hire you. Remember, networking should only be used as a communication process to acquire information, *not* as a manipulation used to acquire power and influence over others. If you are playing the "advice and information game" when you really believe networking is nothing more than the back door route to a new position, you are being insincere, misleading, and ineffective. People who are close to your level of experience, and even those Junior to you or in support positions, can be great sources of information. Be nice to everyone along the way.

Exercise 13: Categorize Your Contacts

List 35 people you believe might be able to assist you in your job hunt and consider how each can help. Divide the list into three categories:

- A: those in a position to hire (this category may be very small);
- B: those in a position to introduce you to others in a position to hire;
- C: those with information or ideas.

It is one thing to understand the concept of networking. It is quite another to *know how* to do it. The good news is that networking is a learnable skill. Start with the easy ones, those friends and colleagues that you feel comfortable calling. Invite them to lunch and say, *"I'm looking for a job and wanted to bounce some ideas off you."* During these initial meetings, you will begin to become more comfortable talking about yourself, and, because these are your friends, they will be more forgiving if you stumble slightly as you refine your marketing message.

For people that you do not know as well, use this four step process: (1) an e-mail, (2) a follow-up phone call, (3) an informational interview, and (4) a follow-up thank you note.

Send an *e-mail* to ask for 15 minutes of their time for advice. Do not put pressure on the individual to find you a job or to interview you. That may be a long-term result, but at this point, an informative conversation should be your objective.

Dear _____:

Jack O'Neill suggested that I contact you about my interest in career opportunities in marketing (in New Jersey, etc.). I am a graduate of XYZ School with experience in...

(Your next paragraph should tell something about your background. Include your prior work experience, abilities, skills, interests, academic history, connection to the geographic region, etc. Your goal is to pique the reader's interest.)

I hope to benefit from the experience and knowledge of others in the field (in New Jersey) who might advise me on opportunities for someone with my qualifications. To help familiarize you with my background, I have taken the liberty of attaching my resume for your review. I would appreciate the opportunity to meet with you for 15 minutes for your guidance. I will call your office next week to see if we can schedule a meeting.

I look forward to discussing my plans with you.

Sincerely,

Your Signature

Your Name Printed

Keep in mind that an e-mail is still a business correspondence. You should use a salutation. Grammar, spelling, and proper punctuation are important. Create a secure e-mail address separate from your current work address or your school address. Yahoo, Google, and your cable provider offer free e-mail accounts. Remember to select a professional name. Partygirl12@gmail.com does not create the impression a job seeker needs to create. All job search–related inquiries should come from this address and it should be checked frequently.

Nothing is more effective than a well-written *email followed by a telephone* call three to five days later. The telephone is the most underutilized tool available to the job seeker. Prepare a script so you can clearly and succinctly introduce yourself and articulate your request. Your ability to present yourself and explain what you hope to gain from meeting with your contacts will determine their response to you. Why have you chosen this particular organization and, more importantly, this particular person to contact over all of the other possibilities? What, specifically, do you want to find out? These types of questions will help you to clarify your objectives in networking before you call or write contacts, and will increase your chances of piquing their interest in meeting you. You must be prepared to say more than *"I am looking for a job and I was wondering if you know of any openings."* Consider instead:

"Hello, Mr./Ms. . This is Sally Smith. I am calling at the suggestion of Jack O'Neill. I sent you a letter last week explaining... (restate the first paragraph of your letter) and I was wondering if you might have 15 minutes next Tuesday or Thursday to meet with me?"

Remember, you do not want to exert pressure on people to find you a job. You only want to explain the purpose of the meeting and articulate how you believe your contacts can be helpful. The objective is to unearth information about them and their job experience.

Choose a private, comfortable setting for making calls. Do not call while you are driving, or from a public place with background noise. Starbucks is a great place to do job-related research, but not to make job related phone calls. Besides your script, keep a pen, pad, and copy of your resume and cover letter at hand. Being prepared will help to ameliorate an attack of phone fright and will prevent you from omitting important information. Your script should include:

- Whom you are calling (address the person by name);
- Who referred you;
- Why you are calling (to determine the status of your letter);
- And, how you believe the person could be helpful.

Your introduction should be brief, listener-centric, and upbeat. As the example suggests, consider giving the listener a choice between something and something, not a choice between something and nothing. For example: *"I was wondering if we might meet Tuesday afternoon or Thursday morning"* is more effective than *"I was wondering if we might meet next week."* Even if both Tuesday and Thursday are not convenient, offering a choice avoids complete rejection and steers your contact into discussing timing. Remember to confirm time and exact address, including floor and room number.

If people seem hesitant to grant your request to meet, clearly state that you are not looking for a job with them and that you are only looking for advice and information. For example:

- **Reluctant Contact:** *"I really don't know of any openings. I'm not sure I can help you."*

  o **Your Response:** *"I appreciate your candor. At this point in my job search, I'm just trying to talk to as many people in the field as possible to get some feedback on my approach and brainstorm where possibilities may exist. I would appreciate it if you could spare 10 minutes for me. Does next Tuesday or Thursday work for you?"*

- **Suspicious Contact:** *"If you are looking for a job, you should contact HR."*

  o **Your Response:** *"Actually, I am not looking for a job at the moment, although I'd be happy to contact HR at a later date. Right now I am eager to meet as many people in the field as possible to get some feedback on my approach and brainstorm where possibilities may exist. I would be grateful if you could spare 10 minutes for me. Does next Tuesday or Thursday work for you?"*

  - **Negative Contact:** *"I can't help you. I'm not the person that you should talk to."*

    OR

    "I don't have time to meet with you."

  o **Your response:** *"Thanks for your candor. Could you suggest someone else I should talk to? Would it be ok if I used your name?"*

If you are still met with resistance, politely bring the conversation to a close and then write a nice thank you email, again stating your intended purpose. Mention your disappointment in not being able to learn from the person's experience and ask to be remembered for future reference. Attach your resume with this email.

Perhaps the greatest challenge when using the telephone is reaching your target. Voice mail has frustrated many job seekers. Be prepared to leave a detailed, but short, message about why you are calling and state a time when you will call back to alert your contact. *Do not simply leave a name and a phone number and expect a person to return your call.*

"Hello, Mr./Ms. . This is Sally Smith. I am calling at the suggestion of Jack O'Neill. I sent you a letter last week explaining... (restate the first paragraph of your letter) and I was hoping to arrange a time to meet with you. I'll call back this afternoon at 3 pm. If that time is not good for you and you would prefer to contact me, I can be reached at 212-555-2222 of JSmith@gmail.com. Thank you, and I look forward to speaking with you."

Be sure to speak slowly and clearly, especially when leaving your phone number.

Reaching receptionists or secretaries can provide a unique set of problems. Keep in mind that it is part of their job to screen phone calls. Secretaries are trained to keep the unwanted world away from a busy boss.

Try to take control of the conversation from the beginning, following your script. Sound confident. If requested to give a reason for the call, offer, *"She is expecting my call. We have corresponded,"* or *"I am calling at the suggestion of Mr. O'Neill."* If your voice conveys uncertainty, you may be giving the secretary just cause to screen you out. *never* try to deceive the secretary by saying, *"I am a friend,"* or *"it is a personal call."* You will only alienate your prospect.

Secretaries can be your best allies, or among your biggest stumbling blocks. Be sure to get their name and establish friendly relationships. Remember, they have access to your target and are likely to share their impressions of you with the boss.

If you doubt that your target will return your call, indicate that you are going out and ask when might be a good time to call again. If after several calls, none have been returned, do not signal exasperation. This will make the secretary defensive. Instead, apologize for calling so often. Ask if you could schedule a phone appointment to break the cycle of telephone tag. The secretary may be moved by your respect for her time and, either schedule a phone appointment, or provide you with information about a better time to call, or, at least, place your message at the top of the pile.

If you cannot get the cooperation of the secretary, try calling before 9 a.m., after 5 p.m., or during lunch when your target person is more likely to answer his or her own phone.

Understand that it may take several attempts over a period of weeks — even months — to get someone's attention. Keep in mind that the way to get a response to any kind of marketing communication is to create multiple, positive impressions.

The Networking Interview

Once you are in your contact's office, it is your responsibility to lead the conversation. You should be prepared to:

- Explain the purpose of the meeting;
- Show how your contact can be helpful;
- Present your background and abilities and skills to put the meeting in context;

- Ask questions to elicit the information you need;
- Present a pleasant, positive demeanor;
- Get the names of others who could be helpful;
- And, be considerate of their time.

The purpose of the meeting is to determine how your abilities, skills, and talents could be used in different settings, so it is important to do a good job presenting them. The ability to communicate your qualifications to potential employers entails more than just informing them of your technical competence. You must be able to illustrate that you have the requisite personal attributes — things like problem solving abilities, analytical skills, assessment, and planning capabilities — to perform the job. The examples that you use to talk about your accomplishments should elucidate your thinking and problem solving style. The more concrete and specific that you are, the better able your contact will be to think of possibilities for you and suggest additional people you should meet. Go back to chapter three and review your examples from the Exercises 8 and 9: *Discover Your Abilities and Skills* and *Catalogue your Achievements*. Again, you see why it is critical to engage in the self-assessment process before launching into the job search process.

A common mistake that people make when networking is to use the meeting as a therapy session. You do not want to inspire guilt, pity or dread. Your goal should be to make your contacts feel good about their ability to help you. It is important that you present yourself as positive, confident and self-assured, not negative, needy and desperate. Never make your contacts feel sorry for you or responsible for your situation. Do not scoff at their suggestions by saying "I've tried that and it does not work"; otherwise your contacts will doubt their ability to help and begin to avoid you. If you need to express anger, bitterness, anxiety, etc., talk to a career coach or seek out a member of the clergy or a sympathetic friend before meeting with your contacts. During your appointments you may want to address:

The careers of the people you are visiting:

- Their background;
- How their interest developed in this area;
- What they like best/least about their work;
- And, their "career steps" (what former jobs they held, what they learned from each, how they progressed from one job to the next).

Advantages and disadvantages of working with that:

- Type of firm, agency or corporation;
- And, geographical area.

The structure of their organization and how it operates:

- Whom they supervise, and to whom they report;
- Performance expectations;
- Advancement opportunities;
- And, future growth potential.

Characteristics the organization values in an employee.

Advice regarding how to make yourself an attractive candidate including suggestions on:

- Upgrading your resume;
- Interviewing techniques;
- Further educational and experiential qualifications you might pursue;

- Additional sources of information;

- And, others in the field with whom you could speak.

- Information about any specific job openings you should consider.

Once contacts get to know you, and you have asked questions about their career (showing genuine interest), it is their prerogative to offer further assistance. Toward the conclusion of your talk, their thoughts might naturally turn to what action they might take on your behalf.

You should express gratitude for offers of assistance and take notes if individuals suggest that you contact colleagues. You might add, *"would it be OK if I use your name when contacting this person?"* If your contacts offer to send out your resumes for you, or make calls on your behalf, make sure you arrange to get a list of those contacted so that you can take control of the follow-up process. Assuming responsibility for the follow-up process will allow your contacts to experience you as efficient and conscientious. If your contacts do not offer assistance or additional names of people to call, you might gently ask if they could suggest names of individuals to speak to who could give you more information.

You may find that the 15 minutes that you asked for stretched to a conversation lasting an hour or more. This usually occurs because people are flattered that you came to them for advice, and are asking about things of importance to them. However, it is up to you to stick to your preset time limit, and let your contacts take the initiative to extend the meeting, if desired.

People love to talk about themselves. This type of conversation tends to be very warm and animated, filled with good will. Even though they may not know of a specific job opening, your contacts are likely to keep you in mind when they do have one; or, when colleagues are trying to fill a position, they may recommend you to them. It is important to stay on their radar screens with periodic updates. While they may want to be helpful, *your* job search is not likely to be their highest priority. It is your responsibility to foster the relationship by staying in touch with them.

When you meet with people on your network list, take notes about the meeting. It would be helpful to start a file for each contact. Be sure to include:

- The contact's name (be sure you have the correct spelling);
- The date of the contact;
- The results of the meeting;
- Follow-up that is required and the timeframe;
- The person who referred you;
- Any personal information that may be helpful;
- And, your impressions of the person and the organization.

The job search process requires that you continually make phone calls, schedule appointments, write follow-up notes, contact new people, etc. It is important to record the dates and times for each activity to remind you what needs to be done. This will help to organize your days, which in turn will allow you to get more accomplished. Use the weekly action plan agenda you created in chapter two.

Follow-up Correspondence

When someone has taken the time to meet with you to provide information, advice, and support, it is necessary and appropriate to send a thank-you note shortly after the meeting. While an e-mail is ok, a handwritten note — in the form of a note card or on your personal stationery — is better. It shows extra effort. Your message should convey gratitude for the time, attention, and guidance shared.

People who help you should be kept apprised of your job search. Remember, the way to get a response to any kind of marketing communication is to create multiple, positive impressions. *Your* job search may not be the most important thing on your contact's mind. If you occasionally can remind people that you are still in the job search, other opportunities may present themselves down the line. It is appropriate to reconnect with people to:

Update and inform. Reconnect with contacts periodically to update them on your job search activities or when new information arises. For example, if your contacts connect you to someone in their network, let them know how the meeting went. Keeping people up to speed is helpful, but do not overdo it. Only contact people if there is truly something of significance to report. If you find yourself calling or e-mailing more than once a week, you have wandered into the "pest" zone. Also, do not worry if your contact does not respond to your e-mail or if you do not speak with the person directly. Leave *a brief* voicemail message with the pertinent information. Do not ask them to return your call. Your goal is to minimize the amount of time and attention you ask of people. Your objective is simply to stay on their radar screen. If you have not had a reason to connect, touch base every four to six weeks to check in.

Solicit information and advice. Call contacts with simple questions. "I just scheduled an interview with 'X,' and was wondering if you might have five minutes to share any insights you might have." These types of solicitation should definitely not be made too often and the questions or guidance should be specific and in instances when their opinion would definitely make a difference. If you are considering asking them which tie to wear to the interview, you have wander into the "pest" zone.

Share information of interest to *them*. Your job search activities may uncover information that may be of interest to your contacts. Perhaps you will learn information about emergent trends, client development opportunities, or something of a personal nature. Make those connections whenever possible.

Finally, remember that you want your contacts to always have a pleasant, positive experience during their interactions with you, so that they will be inspired to refer you to people. It is *never* appropriate to call your contacts to whine or complain. While the job search can be frustrating, use your friends and family, or hire a career coach to help you through the rough patches, *but not* your contacts. Most importantly, remember to let your contacts know when you have landed a position. Thank them again for their support and guidance, and offer your willingness to return the favor.

After each informational interview, review your performance. Did you present your abilities and skills as effectively as possible? Did you craft your questions to elicit the information you needed? What could you have done better?

Organize the information that you have received. Are there new books to read, new resources to consider, additional organizations to explore, or new people to meet? Develop your plan of action based on this new information. Remember, the job search process is circuitous. Information that you uncover while networking may suggest a need to revamp your resume, or open up a new avenue of employers to research.

Informational interviewing requires a long term view, strategic planning, and a commitment to working at it. It takes patience and perseverance to use this process to uncover job opportunities, but it is the most effective method to find a professional job.

CHAPTER SIX

STEP 5: CULTIVATE YOUR NETWORK

Because the Internet makes it easy to "connect" with people, many job hunters over use it and ignore the importance of face-to-face interactions. Being "linked to" or "friends with" someone is only the first step. You must take actions to nurture those relationships throughout your career, not just when you need something from them. And while relationships can be maintained or fostered easily enough online, human interaction is critical to making a positive connection last. You must be fearless about meeting people live.

In chapter five, the focus was on networking with people that you know. Now, we must focus on who you *need* to know. Anxiety often causes people to talk themselves out of participating in worthwhile networking activities that will enable them to meet new people and increase their visibility. The fear of walking into the office of someone that they do not know or into a room filled with senior managers or total strangers is pervasive, cutting across boundaries of age, sex, race, socioeconomic level, and professional and personal experience. But do whatever it takes to silence those discouraging voices in your head and motivate yourself to go anyway. Reassure yourself that once you are at the meeting or event, you will be fine. And, in the worse-case scenario, if you are truly as miserable as those little voices in your head said that you would be, you can always leave.

Challenge the myths you accepted as a child that may impede your ability to network effectively.

Myth One: **It is impolite to talk about yourself.**

We have grown up believing that it is tacky to use people for personal gain. Being polite means being unobtrusive, not asking direct questions, not talking about our personal lives, and drawing as little attention to ourselves as possible.

Reality: You have many things to *offer* as well as to gain. By freely acknowledging that attending an event is good for you because it will provide you with the opportunity to mingle with senior executives, to develop business, to meet potential employers, or simply because it feels good to support a cause, you will eliminate the feeling of "dishonesty" and "tackiness" and be able to enjoy the event and participate fully. The networking opportunities will develop naturally.

Myth Two: **Do not talk to strangers.**

Ever since childhood, parents instilled a fear about talking to people we did not know.

Reality: Consider the old saying: "strangers are friends that we have not met yet." Think about what you have in common with others in the room. Are they members of the same industry, alumni, parents, church members, or supporters of a political candidate? Determining the common bond makes it easier to approach people because they are no longer "strangers." You can then begin a conversation based on the common bond.

Myth 3: **Wait until you are properly introduced.**

Reality: Because it is not always feasible to be introduced by a mutual acquaintance, you may need to "properly introduce" yourself. Use your marketing statement from chapter three to create a two to three sentence self-introduction that is clear, interesting, and well-delivered. Your goal is to tell people who you are in a pleasant, positive manner. Naturally, what you say will depend on the nature of the event. For example:

- At a company function: *"I recognize you from the elevator. I am Kate Currie from the marketing department."*

- At an industry convention: *"Hello, my name is Kate Currie. I am the Chief Marketing Officer at XYZ company."*

- At a wedding: *"Hello. I do not believe that we have met. I am Kate Currie, former college roommate of the bride."*

Fear of rejection often stands in the way of approaching new people. This particular obstacle is more imagined than real. Very few people will be openly hostile or rude, if for no other reason than that it is bad manners. To help overcome this fear, try adopting a "host mentality." Hosts are concerned with the comfort of others and actively contribute to that comfort. By focusing on making others feel welcomed and included, you will become more comfortable. Find the person standing alone and introduce yourself. That person will likely be grateful. But, even if you *are* met with rudeness, do not take it personally. Such behavior reveals more about the other person than it does about you. There may be a hundred reasons why that person is not receptive. Simply move on.

The best networkers put people at ease from the outset, and that makes conversations flow naturally. People who are most successful at it are those who genuinely like people. There is nothing calculated or manipulative about attending events to meet people. Remind yourself what has brought this particular group of people together, and why it is important for you to be there.

Mastering the art of small talk will ease any prevailing networking anxieties and is simple to do. If you read a newspaper, or watch the News, you are ready for small talk. Use your observational skills to spark a lively, personal exchange. Consider one of the following three methods to get a conversation started.

- **Share an observation**. Comment on a current, relevant news event, or the situation at hand. Remark on the facility, food, organization, traffic, parking dilemma, etc. Remember, the comment ought to be positive and upbeat. Look for those bridges that have led the two of you to be in the same room.

- **Ask an open-ended question.** (Examples: *"How long have you been a member of this organization?" "How do you fit into this picture?" "How do you know the bride or groom?")* Be careful not to fire off too many questions; you want to engage people in a conversation, not make them feel like they are being interrogated.

- **Reveal something about yourself**. Disclosing something about you helps to establish vulnerability and approachability. (Example: *"I have worked here for 3 months and have never been to the 48th floor."*) Volunteering information about yourself will make the other person feel safe about doing the same. Be careful not to reveal anything too personal that may burden the listener. (Example: *"My spouse just asked me for a divorce."*)

There is a natural rhythm to small talk. It should be interactive. After the initial introduction, the flow is *probe, response, comment.*

Example (at an industry event):

- Introduce: "I don't believe we've met. I'm Mary Reilly."

- Probe: "Which organization are you with?"

- Response: *"I'm Jack De Mario, with ABC Corporation."*
- (Mary) Comment: "I've heard great things about ABC."
- Probe: "What is your role there?"
- (Jack) Response: "I am with the marketing group."
- (Mary) Comment: "I just graduated with a degree in marketing."
- Probe: "Does your company use social media to reach clients?"

Even if the other person does not ask you any probing questions, you will be able to move the conversation forward. Naturally, the comment and follow-up probe should be based on what was said.

In any networking situation, it is wise to ask great questions and get others to do most of the talking. This way, you will learn valuable information about the other person and their jobs. Assuming Mary Reilly is looking for a job in marketing, the conversation is likely to flow based on their mutual interests. If Jack De Mario was with a group Mary had little interest in, it would still be wise to continue the conversation with a few probing questions.

- Introduce: "I don't believe we've met. I'm Mary Reilly."
- Probe: "Which organization are you with?"
- Response: *"I'm Jack De Mario, with ABC Corporation."*
- (Mary) Comment: "I've heard great things about ABC."
- Probe: "What is your role there?"
- (Jack) Response: "I am the head of risk management."
- (Mary) Comment: "I have heard the term "risk management" a lot throughout college, but I have to admit, I am not really sure what it entails."
- Probe: "What kinds of things is your department responsible for?"

Not every conversation will lead to a new connection or a job opportunity. However, genuine curiosity is enough to keep the conversation flowing. At some point, Jack is likely to ask Mary, *"where do you work?"* or *"what do you do?"* and she can respond, *"I just graduated XYZ University with a degree in Marketing, and I am looking to join a company interested in growing its social media presence. Does your company use social media?"* Jack may offer to introduce Mary to the head of marketing at his company or he may simply say, *"I have no idea."* Allow the conversation to come to a natural close, and move on.

The objective of attending an event is to meet a number of people. It is important to circulate. Do not monopolize any one person's time, and do not allow your time to be monopolized by any one person. If someone has latched on to you, choose whether or not you want to make it your responsibility to take care of him/her throughout the event, thereby missing other opportunities present in the room. It is not rude to move on. To make an exit, offer a connecting gesture like a handshake, or a pat on the arm or shoulder, and simply say:

- *"I am sure that there are other people that you need to talk to. I do not want to monopolize your time. It has been interesting speaking with you."*

- *"Excuse me, it was nice meeting you."*

- *"Excuse me; there is someone that I need to say hello to."* (Make sure you move to another part of the room.)

To join the next group, simply say:

- *"Excuse me for interrupting, but I wanted to say hello."*

Another option would be to position yourself close to a group already engaged in conversation. Avoid groups that appear to be engaged in private, intimate conversations. Give facial feedback to comments. When you feel included (usually after you have established eye contact with someone in the group), feel free to join the conversation.

Remember to be open to others who may want to join a group that you are already a part of. If you are doing the introductions, remember to "introduce up." Bluntly put, that means to introduce the person with the lesser title to the person with the higher title.

If there *is* something you want from someone you meet, decide whether it is appropriate to ask at that moment, or if it would be sufficient to exchange information and follow-up at a later date. Often times, the latter is the better option. Say *"I would love to learn more about how you use social media, but I do not want to monopolize your time here. Would it be ok if I contact you next week to set up a time to meet?"*

Jot notes on the back of business cards to ensure that you remember what was discussed. Send an invitation via LinkedIn to build the relationship. (Remember to send a personalized invitation.) Keep in mind, the person who collects the most business cards *is not* the winner. If you are simply collecting cards, you likely have not established an impression, and it is likely the person will not remember you after the event.

Business cards are a must in order to facilitate the exchange of information with people that you meet. If you are currently a student, or are unemployed, create a personal card containing your name, phone, and email address. Place your cards in an easy to reach place. You may want to invest in an attractive card carrying case. Once you have established rapport and decided that you are interested in exchanging cards, offer yours first. People will typically return in kind. If they do not, you could also ask if they are on LinkedIn and send them a personalized invitation the next day.

Finally, you are completely responsible for what you bring into a room or meeting, and for what you project onto other people. Think about how other people see you. Are you living by your life rules? Inferences about your abilities are based on the image that you project.

People are judged not only by the words that they choose to articulate thought, but also by the tone and body language used during the delivery. Competence is inferred by the way we speak about what we know. It is important to be mindful of the images you project, not so as to live up to the images of others, but to ensure that any inferences made about you accurately reflect who you are. To do so, you must develop effective communication skills. (Refer to chapter nine.) This is not to suggest that form is more important than substance. However, you do not want your "form" to impede your ability to project competency.

Perception *is* reality. If you look and act like you have already lost, or someone who does not belong, that is exactly how people will respond to you. Your facial expression, posture, and willingness to launch conversations matter. Your body language plays an important role in how people receive your message. To leverage your non-verbal assets and make certain your body always supports your message, consider the following tips.

Dress for success. Business casual has created distinct challenges in today's workplace. It is more difficult to define what dressing for success looks like. To state the obvious, your look should always be neat, ironed and professional. Pay attention to the details: hair, nails, shoe shine, etc. The packaging is important.

Make eye contact. Look people directly in the eye when you are speaking. This serves three purposes: 1) it demonstrates confidence, and you appear in control; 2) it engages people (your eyes are like magnets; people cannot look away. They will feel acknowledged and drawn in to the conversation.); and 3) it provides instant feedback to determine how your message is being received. You will be able to see if people are confused, doubtful, bored, etc., and adjust your message accordingly.

Use your body to project confidence. Your stance should convey power and authority. Stand tall with your shoulders back and your feet firmly planted about hip width apart. This will allow you to balance your weight and minimize distracting shifts from leg to leg, as well as rocking backing and forth or swaying, which makes you look nervous and uncomfortable.

Understand the power of your voice. Your voice is a very powerful, though seldom thought about, tool. Notice effective speakers. There is a pace and a rhythm to their speech patterns. They project their voices, use pauses for dramatic effect, and always manage to have a conversational tone to better connect with the people with whom they are speaking. Speak slowly, enunciate clearly, and smile when appropriate to let your enthusiasm and energy come through.

Be mindful of word choice. There is never a need for expletives, racial epithets, or sexually charged language. Also, be mindful of how you use words such as "like," "you know," and other colloquialisms. They signal a lack of polish and professionalism. And whatever you do, avoid calling anyone "dude" or "bro."

Remember to breathe. If your speech pattern is peppered with "ums," "uhs," "ers," "you knows" and "likes," it is likely because you are nervous and are not breathing properly. At the end of each sentence, take a breath, focus your eyes, and deliver the next sentence or thought. Power is never rushed.

Remember, communication involves the intentions and actions of the speaker as well as the interpretations of the listener. While the person delivering the message knows exactly what is meant to be conveyed, the words chosen and the manner used to present the information may support or completely negate the intent. And sometimes, no matter how clearly the intended message was presented, listeners receive information through their own set of filters, which may distort the intended message and result in miscommunication.

You cannot control how other people share or process information. But you can consider their style and adapt your own style to improve communication. The purpose of adjusting your style to others is not simply to be nice. It is more self-serving than that. By giving your listeners *what they* need, you are more likely to get *what you* need from the exchange. For example, is your listener a fast moving, action-oriented extrovert, or a quiet, thoughtful introvert? Is this someone who likes detail and information, or only bottom line information? Is this someone with whom you can think out loud or someone who only wants to hear the end decision? Answers to these questions can help you adjust your approach.

Dress and behave like a professional; be positive and upbeat; project a proud, confident image. Radiate confidence and people will be naturally drawn to you in every situation throughout your career. That will help to ensure that you have limitless resources in place when you need them.

Exercise 14: Attend an Event

Challenge yourself to attend a relevant professional event. Consider an alumni function, association meeting, or community event; any place where you do not know many attendees. Practice your networking skills by making it a goal to meet three new people, and strategize how to build the relationship after the event.

CHAPTER SEVEN

STEP 6: UNDERSTAND THE JOB SEARCH PROCESS

The Internet is a great tool, and it has made job hunting both easier and more difficult. It is easier to find opportunities and apply quickly to a wider audience without the cost of expensive resume paper, matching envelopes, and postage. However, because it is easier to apply, job seekers often apply to everything with little thought about finding the right match. They join "talent" communities, set up search agents, link to or friend everyone that they can, and spend the majority of their job search hours on the computer. Then, after applying to thousands of positions and receiving no interviews, job seekers get discouraged and ultimately quit trying.

To mitigate these difficulties, you must use online applications in conjunction with every other resource available to you in order to be effective. Sitting home in your pajamas applying to jobs online without doing any follow-up is not likely to yield the results that you want. Applying online is just the first step.

To find jobs online, start with the broad search engines such as www.careerbuilders.com or www.indeed.com. Their drop down menus and search tools will typically lead you to niche websites or company websites. (Revisit Exercise 5 in chapter two. Also, visit the Appendix).

If you can apply directly through a company website, you should. Studies show they have a higher rate of return than applying to job boards. If you are having a difficult time locating the career section of a particular company, google "jobs at (company name)" and scan the results to find the page that has the company name in the URL. (It is usually not at the top of the search.)

Some career pages are easier to navigate than others. The easier ones allow you to download a resume and cover letter, answer a few EEOC questions, and you are done. Others will allow you to download your resume, but they also want you to fill out a form that covers the very information found on your resume. You must fill in those forms to increase your chances of having your attached resume reviewed. It is time consuming and annoying, but absolutely necessary. Some websites will allow you to download your resume and it automatically fills in the form for you. However, make sure that you review all the information to ensure that it translated properly. (It does not always.)

Finally, there are those websites that require you to answer prescreening questions. These present a unique challenge because the questions are often written for a wide range of positions within the company and do not always make sense in the context of the position for which you are applying. Again, it is time consuming and annoying to answer these questions, but necessary if you want to be considered for the position.

The most challenging websites require you to answer a laundry list of questions in order to apply for a position. The Government refers to this section as SKA (Skills, Knowledge, and Abilities), but the questions come in a wide variety of shapes and forms. Some want you to write paragraphs to answer questions while others offer you limited drop down options. The questions with the asterisk require responses while the others do not. Be as truthful and as thorough as possible when answering the questions; however, when the question is vague, always give yourself the benefit of the doubt in interpreting the question and crafting your response.

The hardest question to address is the salary question. If they ask "what is your current salary," there is no way to reframe the question so, if the question has an asterisk, you must give them the information in order to proceed. If it allows you to leave it blank, do that and deal with the question during the interview. If they ask "what salary range are you seeking," you should visit www.payscale.com and complete the "what if" scenario to come up with a realistic range. Again, if you can proceed without supplying a number, that is the best option.

Whichever type of website you encounter, be prepared to invest at least 30 - 45 minutes to complete the application. If you are in a rush, bookmark the page and complete the application when you have time. Many websites will not allow you to save an incomplete application and return later.

According to the Society of Human Resource Managers (SHRM), computers read your resume first, not a human being. Software is designed to search for specific words, so format your electronic resume to work for you by investing the time to tailor it to specific positions. At least 75% of online resumes are discarded for using the wrong words. Incorporate the language used in the job postings to describe your experiences. This means that you must tailor your resume for each position.

SHRM also indicates that more than 20% of resumes are screened out due to formatting issues. (This is why it is so important to incorporating networking into your job search.) To avoid this issue, use the *Save As* function on your computer to create a second version of your resume in ASCII text or Rich Text Format to eliminate all the underlining, italics, and graphics on your resume. These are easier to use when posting resumes in on-line databases. You will only need to proofread the new document once to ensure that the information is translated properly during the reformatting process. Then, you can cut and paste the document into the online database.

Even if a cover letter is optional, include one. Its purpose is to support your candidacy by supplementing the information set forth in your resume and offer the employer a glimpse of your personality. A cover letter should:

- Convince the reader that you are worth getting to know better;

- Draw attention away from liabilities by addressing potential questions that the resume may raise;

- Emphasize salient achievements and accomplishments in greater depth than the resume does;

- Introduce new sales material that is not included on your resume;

- And, demonstrate enthusiasm and knowledge of the industry.

A cover letter is the ideal place to focus on the specific abilities and skills you want to emphasize for a particular employer. Some general guidelines for writing good cover letters include:

- Use correct grammar, good sentence structure and standard business letter format.

- State the purpose of your letter. If you are responding to an advertisement, indicate the source. If you are writing at the suggestion of a mutual acquaintance, indicate that immediately. Cover letters should be slanted as individually as possible.

- Pinpoint how your abilities, skills, and experience relate to the particular needs of the employer to whom you are writing. Focus your letter on the needs of the reader. Focus on what you can do for the employer. Which credentials, abilities, skills, and experience do you have that would help the employer? No one cares what the job would do for you.

- Always be objective when describing yourself to an employer. For example, instead of writing *"I am a hard worker," "I would be a great asset to your firm"* or *"I have many leadership qualities,"* show them by means of examples from your past: *"The experience I gained as director of the office is indicative of my leadership abilities."*

- Address your letter to a specific person by name and title whenever possible. You may need to do some research to identify the proper person.

- Limit your cover letter to three or four paragraphs. It should rarely be more than one page.

- Present unique or distinctive attributes, without using superlatives, in an attractive, professional, and well-written manner.

- Close your cover letter with a request for an interview indicating what action you will take - i.e., that you will call them (within 7-10 days) to arrange a meeting. Then, follow through.

- Keep careful records of the positions for which you have applied. Maintain copies of your correspondence with dates indicating when you will follow-up. *Follow-up* is crucial.

Exercise 15: Craft a Cover Letter

First paragraph: Mention the name of any person who referred you to this employer first, if this information is available to include. Otherwise, start your letter with a powerful statement that will grab the reader's attention. Identify yourself and the type of position you are seeking. State how you heard about this job opening. *("As a summa cum laude graduate at Princeton with a B.S. in Economics, I am writing in response to your posting on Careerbuilders for X job.")*

Second paragraph: Explain why you are qualified for or interested in this particular position. Stress how you can benefit the employer and what you have to offer to them. Do not repeat word for word the text of your resume. Rather, highlight and embellish upon the most significant aspects of your background with regard to that particular employer. Consider using bullets to draw attention to your accomplishments. If you are responding to an ad, try to use the language used in the ad to describe your experience.

Third paragraph *(optional)*: If you are applying for a position in a different geographic location, explain your ties to or interest in that locale.

Fourth paragraph: Restate your interest in the particular organization, and express your desire for an interview. State how the employer may contact you if your address and phone number are different from the information on your resume. You may also state that you will call to set up an appointment. If you are truly interested in this job, feel free to take the initiative.

Your cover letter can be a separate document, or it can be the body of your email, if you are applying directly and not through an online database. Be sure to include a salutation and signature.

If you choose to post your resume in a searchable database, make sure there is a confidentiality feature so that your contact information will not be distributed until you agree to release it to a specific employer. Also, make sure those resumes are dated so that you can confirm that your resume is the most current version.

After you have submitted your application, you still have work to do. Review the list of contacts that you developed in chapters five and six. Does anyone work at the organization to which you have just applied? Do not assume that, because you discussed your career goals with them earlier, they will automatically think of you. Reach out to the person.

- *"Jack, I wanted to let you know that I applied to the X position that your company advertised on its webpage this morning. I would appreciate any tips that you might have on how I can secure an interview."*

Even if no one on your list works at the target company, consider the possibility that someone on your contact list knows someone who works at the organization to which you have applied. Use the "search by company" function on LinkedIn to identify useful second level connections. Reconnect with your contact and remind them you are actively looking. Contact that person and say something like:

- **To a contact with a known connection to the employer:**
- *"I wanted to let you know that I applied for a position at XYZ Corporation advertised on Ccareer builder. I remembered that they are a client of yours. Would you be comfortable introducing me?"* **Or** *"Do you know anyone in the sales department that I could follow up with?"*
- **To other contacts**: *"I applied to a position at XYZ Corporation, and wanted to see if you knew anyone there."*
- **To a LinkedIn connection:** *"I saw that you are connected to Joe Smith at ABC Corporation. I just applied to a position there and would appreciate it if you would introduce me so that I can follow-up on my application."*

Let us assume that you do not know anyone with a connection to the employer. Get creative. Look at investor relations page on the company website to see who is on the Board of Directors that you or one of your contacts might know. Check out LinkedIn "search by company" function to see if you can find the name of someone in Human Resources, or the department that you are interested in, to follow up with. Return to the library and look at Reference USA Business Directors online, ESBCO Business Source, or EBSCO Regional Business Source to uncover a name. You could upgrade to LinkedIn's Premium Package that allows you to send InMails to people that you are not linked to. Even if you do not know the person or anyone who can introduce you, send that person and email or letter introducing yourself, and express an interest in the role.

You could also search the phrase *"Human Resources Director at XYZ Company"* in Google to see if you can uncover a name or call the organization's general number and ask for the proper spelling of the head of Human Resources department or the department in which you have an interest. Do not ask to *speak* with that person. It will be obvious that it is a solicitation of some sort. Make two phone calls. That way, when you call back later in the day and ask for Mary Jones, your call will be less suspect and you will have a greater chance of getting through. Follow up directly with that person to ensure that your resume has been received, and ask if there is any additional information that you can supply. Always take the *"how can I be helpful to you"* approach rather than the *"why haven't you called me in for an interview yet?"* approach.

Finally, when it comes to online resumes, think before you submit. Wait a day, review the job posting again, and decide if it is a good fit before you apply. Do not wait several days, or even weeks, or the job might disappear, but do allow yourself a short amount of time to consider your qualifications for the position and your strategy for both applying and following-up. It is the quality of the applications that makes the difference, not the quantity. Keep in mind, ads are written for the *"perfect"* candidate and the *"perfect"* candidate rarely exists. If you possess 60% of the stated qualifications, consider applying.

Like job hunting online, working with recruiters can be both a positive and a negative. Candidates who come through a recruiter come with a huge price tag, usually about a third of the candidate's first year salary. By using your contacts to stay in the information loop and uncovering openings, you can approach employers directly, thereby eliminating the fee and making yourself a more attractive candidate. However, with that said, it is still important for job seekers to learn how to incorporate headhunters into their job search activities.

Because it is the headhunters' business to know what is happening in the marketplace, they can provide valuable information about things like which academic and professional credentials are hot, and which geographic regions have increasing opportunities. They generally do not work with entry-level candidates, but if a recruiter calls you, take the call. Keep an open mind, at least long enough to hear the pitch and see what you can learn.

Before you decide to proceed with a headhunter, ask what procedures will be followed, as well as what precautions will be taken to ensure your privacy and maintain the confidentiality of all transactions. Generally, the process follows a similar pattern. First, you will be interviewed by the headhunter to determine what you are looking for, and if any suitable positions currently exist. If so, you will be asked for your permission to send your resume to the employer. Do not give blanket approval to distribute your resume everywhere, particularly if you are working with several recruiters. That could create a fee dispute and cause problems for the employer, and ultimately for you. If you learn of an opening independently, do not let the headhunter send your resume. Send it yourself to avoid the price tag unless the company indicates they will only accept resumes through their designated headhunter.

The headhunter's task is to present your credentials in such a way as to entice the employer to want to meet you. Provide the headhunter with as much relevant information as possible to make that step easy. Once that is accomplished, you can expect multiple interviews with the employer. If the employer determines that you are the candidate that he wants to hire, you will begin salary negotiations through the headhunter.

It is important to remember that the fee-paying employer is the headhunter's "client," while you are merely the "candidate." The role of the headhunter *is not* to help you find a job; it is to help his or her client successfully fill a position. The headhunter always works for the employer, and is paid to tend to the client's interest. The headhunter is not your friend, or your therapist. This is a business relationship, so the information that you choose to share is critical to how you will be presented to his or her client.

The bottom line that, is once you have applied for a position - whether on line or through a recruiter - you want to talk to as many people in your network as possible to make sure that your resume is noticed, and you land the interview.

CHAPTER EIGHT

STEP 7: GET THE OFFER: INTERVIEW STRATEGIES THAT WORK

The basic question in every interview is *"why should I hire you?"* Your objective is to translate your abilities, skills, and attributes into benefits for the *employer*. It is now time to fully implement the winning formula that we discussed in chapter two: Self-Assessment + Market Assessment = Career Success! You must be able to verbalize *why* your strengths are of *value* to this specific employer. Do not expect your past experience to speak for itself; be prepared to state the obvious.

The recruiter's objective is to assess your credentials, form an impression about your personality, and determine the degree to which your interests and background correspond with the employer's hiring needs. Your background and record of accomplishments are amplified or diminished in the eyes of the recruiter by the general impression that you create. Again, this is not to suggest that form is more important than substance; however, you want to ensure that the form that you present does not create any barriers that prevent the employer from experiencing your substance.

The first few minutes of the interview are crucial. Employers make up their mind about candidates very early. Your handshake must be firm and confident, your gaze steady, your appearance impeccable, and your confidence must be apparent. Throughout the interview, decision makers are searching for clues that address the following questions:

- Can you do the job?
- Do you interact with people easily?
- Are you easy to interview; are you confident and clear in your answers?
- Do you listen?
- Do you ask sensible questions?
- Are you likeable?
- Will you complement or disrupt the department?
- Do you demonstrate good judgment?

Interviewers typically use one of five interviewing methods to learn about candidates. Understanding the differences among these interviewing styles and preparing a strategy to effectively deal with each of them will improve your chances for success.

1. **Behavioral Interview**. Precise questions designed to elicit specific information about how your accomplishments demonstrate the behaviors that have proven successful at their organization are asked. The questions are formulated from the contents of your resume. *Strategy:* Answers should be brief, and should objectively emphasize *how* you achieved concrete accomplishments. Be concise, but do not fall into the trap of responding with monosyllabic yes or no answers. Review the company website to get a sense of the behaviors important to the organization, and select stories that demonstrate success in those areas.

2. **Nondirective Interview**. The recruiter's intent is to get the candidate to do all the talking. This usually does not work to your advantage. Your goal should be to get the recruiter to do at

least 50% of the talking. *Strategy:* Construct a narrative history of yourself related to the position in advance to enable you to make a clear, concise statement explaining your value. Attempt to draw the recruiter into the conversation by asking questions.

3. **Free Wheeling Interview**. This type of interview lacks any semblance of structure or direction. Since many managers have limited interviewing experience, they have no tactical plan. *Strategy*: Control the flow of the conversation by opening the interview with highlights of your accomplishments, and then move directly into your own questions. This helps put the recruiter at ease and helps to focus him/her on your assets.

4. **Hypothetical or Problem Solving Interview**. During this type of interview, the employer will pose an industry specific problem to solve. They are trying to determine your technical knowledge. Oftentimes, they are less concerned about you having the "right" answer and more concerned about your problem solving process. *Strategy*: Take a moment to consider the question. Do not be afraid of silence. It demonstrates thoughtfulness. Demonstrate that you can spot the issues and indicate where/how you would approach the problem.

5. **Stress Interview**. This is perhaps the most difficult interview of all. Its purpose is to measure your poise and emotional stability. The recruiter tries to appear curt, argumentative, and/or impatient, firing questions in rapid succession. The questions may be designed to bait you into a topical argument. *Strategy:* Remain patient and calm. Indicating annoyance, tension or nervousness serves no purpose. To avoid a debate, try to change the topic by asking a question. Remember, this type of interview is designed to rattle you.

While it is natural to be nervous in interviews, your goal is to focus on your message, not on your nerves. Remember, you would not be approaching this meeting at all if you were not qualified for the position. Your thorough preparation has made you aware of both your strengths and your weaknesses. But remember, the interviewer is there to see what you have to offer, not to hear explanations about what you do not have. When you practice answering interview questions, eliminate all instances of "no," "not," "didn't," "although," "but," and "however" from your speech. Rephrase your answers using positive speech forms. This will prepare you to speak about yourself in a positive light.

Think of at least three main points that you want to make. Use concrete and clear examples that demonstrate these strengths. Focus on these identified strengths during the interview, and present them with conviction and enthusiasm. Remember that the interviewer must be able to see and hear the enthusiasm that you wish to portray.

Try to anticipate the types of questions that you will be asked, and prepare multilevel responses. Write out your answers. Review and edit them. First, give a brief summary, akin to a verbal outline, covering all salient points. Second, pause to gauge the interest of the interviewer and give a more detailed description if the interviewer seems interested, or asks you to go on. Be certain that your responses highlight your abilities and skills, demonstrate your knowledge and expertise, and reflect your motivation and personality. Even if you believe that it is obvious that you are highly qualified for the position, take time to collect your thoughts and think about your answers.

Exercise 16: Plan the Interview

Write out the answers to the following questions.

1. What are the three points that I must make at some time during our conversation?

2. What are my most marketable abilities and skills?

3. What are the abilities and skills that I most want to use in my next job?

4. What is the question that I am most afraid of being asked? How will I respond?

5. What are the aspects (tendencies, interview abilities, comfort level, specific questions I am nervous about being asked) of the interview situation on which I most need to work?

Exercise 17: Craft Responses to Interview Prep Questions

Rehearse your answers to the following questions.

- Tell me about yourself. (What they are really asking here is, "what in your background makes you a good candidate for this job?")

- What are your long and short term goals and objectives? (Be sure to make the connection between your goals and this job for which you are interviewing.)

- What do you see yourself doing five years from now? (Again, tie your answer into the position available. Never, ever say that you want to be doing something unrelated.)

- Which two or three accomplishments have given you the most satisfaction? Why? (Talk about specific projects, especially if they are relevant to the position.)

- In what ways do you think you can make a contribution to our firm/company?

- In what sort of environment are you most comfortable? (Your favorite environment should be similar to that of the employer with whom you are interviewing.)

- Why do you want to work with our company/firm? (Be specific. Show that you have done your research. Make sure the interviewer knows that you understand their business.)

- What do you consider to be the strongest qualities in your personality and character? (List about three and relate them to the job opening.)

- I see from your resume that you (play basketball or speak French or are interested in real estate, etc. This is not a statement where you answer "yes" or "no." Hear this as: tell me more about ....)

- What else do you think that I should know about you? (From your preparation beforehand, you will have an additional strength or accomplishment that you will want to highlight here. Do not say there is not anything else. You are more exciting than that.)

Identify every question that you may dread being asked. Prepare a succinct answer for each. Practice saying the answer aloud. Go over each question and response repeatedly until you are desensitized to the stress that each causes.

If you believe negative assumptions are being made about you (e.g., that you are too young to be taken seriously, too old to take supervision from someone junior, or lack a specific skill set, etc.), address the elephant in the room by offering evidence to assuage their fears and prove that their assumptions are not true. But, proceed with caution. You do not want to highlight a "problem" that the employer does not have with your candidacy. (Review your NAILs from chapter two).

Before you walk in the door, obtain information about the employer from as many sources as possible. You do not want to waste valuable time asking questions that can easily be answered by reading the employer's website, or by doing a Google search. The more information that you have before the interview, the better you will be able to make a compelling connection between your abilities and skills, and the employer's needs.

Assemble your interview kit. It should contain:

- Contact information and directions to the interview;
- Extra copies of your resume;
- Transcripts, portfolio, or writing samples;
- Reference list or letters.

Expect the unexpected so that you will not be rattled if things do not go according to plan. Interviewers may change, you may meet more people than expected, or client demands may affect the appointment time. And remember, every question counts. Something as innocent as, "Did you have any trouble finding us?" could start the interview off on a bad note if you carry on about traffic or bad directions.

During the interview, you must:

- **Establish rapport**. In addition to tangible things such as a good, firm handshake, and appropriate eye contact, there are additional items that develop rapport between people. These include friendliness and sincere interest in the interviewer, as well as warmth and responsiveness. You must become aware of body language. Be sensitive to cues of boredom. If the interviewer keeps looking down at your resume or out the window, bring the statement that you are making to a close.

- **Listen carefully**. Try to hear the question behind the question and respond to the interviewer's concerns. Get the interviewer to talk about the position to uncover exactly what is being sought. This will enable you to illustrate how you can fill these needs.

- **Ask questions**. Remember, this is a conversation; there should be interaction. Ask technical questions to demonstrate your knowledge of the field, and to show that you are already looking for solutions to the employer's problems. *Do not* ask about benefits, vacations, pensions, and hours until you know that you have an offer. However, be prepared to answer questions about salary and benefits if posed by the interviewer. (Refer back to chapter two for tips on how to handle the salary question.)

- **Get feedback.** Before the end of the interview, ask if you have the qualifications that they are seeking. If not, now is the best time to find out so that you can adjust your approach.

- **Take control of the follow-up process.** When interviewers indicate that they will "let you know," ask if you can call on a specific day in the future. This may help to accelerate the decision making process. Also, let them know if you have other offers.

- **Maintain a positive attitude.** Adopt a "have done - can do - will do" attitude. It is not always what you say that counts, but how you say it. View anything negative as a challenge, an opportunity, and something exciting. Do not be apologetic about anything; handle your "Achilles' heel" factually and non-defensively.

You can help an inexperienced interviewer feel more comfortable by asking questions. Your prepared questions can demonstrate your knowledge of the field and your interest in the employer, and provide the interviewer with an opportunity to relax by talking about something with which he or she is familiar. You can ask things like:

- *"What do you see as the growth areas of the company?"*
- *"What products are likely to do well in the next few years?"*
- *"What criteria are used to evaluate performance?"*
- *"What role does the position play in helping the company achieve its mission?"*
- *"What are the five most important duties?"*
- *"From a management perspective, which skills or attributes do you think are most important?"*

If you believe negative assumptions are being made about you, confidently address the issue in order to eliminate the perceptions.

- *"During other interviews, I have been asked about (my ability to accept supervision from someone younger than I am, limited experience in X, or my commitment to this geographic area), and we haven't talked about that yet."* Deliver a positive statement to address those concerns.

By offering questions that allow the interviewer to relax and think about the answers, the interview becomes a freer exchange of information. This benefits all the parties involved. You will appear more confident, and the interviewer will feel more comfortable in your presence and will be more likely to recommend you. Your questions should not convey an undue concern over salary, time off, or any of the more mundane aspects of the job. Stay interested in important aspects such as challenge, responsibility, and those that show a mature and forward-thinking mentality. The dollars and cents concerns can be ironed out after an offer has been made.

Hiring decisions tend to be based on somewhat subjective material. Unfortunately, trying to determine if someone "fits in" to a particular environment can lead to subtle forms of discrimination. While interviewers typically try to avoid asking personal questions, most want to know all that they can about the applicants. Help them by providing information that you are comfortable with discussing and would like the interviewer to know. The information that you volunteer about yourself will be different from what every other applicant offers, and it will help you stand out in the crowd. A word of caution: do not allow yourself to be lured into intimate chitchat. Regardless of the kindness of the interviewer, nothing is "off the record." Keep your comments job-related and, if you can complement your resume in any way by adding something, do it.

Applicants who are not aware of what questions should and should not be asked are more likely to be victims of discrimination. The general rule of thumb is, if the information is not specifically job-related, it should not be asked. Examples of potentially *sensitive* — though not necessarily *unlawful* — subjects include:

- Name origin;
- Residence;
- Age;
- Birthplace;
- Military service;
- National origin;
- Sex;
- Marital status;
- family size;
- Race;
- Color;
- Physical description (i.e., the "tall one," "the blonde one" etc.);
- Physical condition;
- Photograph;
- Religion;
- Arrest record;
- Criminal record;
- Or, fraternal membership.

How the question is posed can determine its lawfulness. For example, asking *"are you a U.S. Citizen?"* or *"where were you born?"* is different from asking you *"Are you authorized to work in the U.S.?"* Similarly, while it is acceptable for an employer to inquire *"Are you willing to relocate?"* it is not acceptable for him or her to attempt to infer the answer to that by asking *"are you married?"*

In most states, there are laws that render some questions illegal; the general results being that an employer should not ask:

- If the applicant has worked under another name;

- The maiden name of the wife or mother of the applicant;

- An applicant to take a pre-employment physical examination, or to inquire about the nature and severity of physical or mental handicaps;

- About marital plans, arrangements for child care, current or anticipated pregnancy status;

- About the occupations of spouses, parents, or siblings;

- For information relating to family background that may reveal race, ethnicity, religion, citizenship and/or national origin;

- About holidays observed or membership in clubs, churches and fraternities;

- About languages written, spoken, or read, unless the employer is specifically seeking to hire someone with that particular skill;

- For proof of age;

- Or, for a photograph prior to the interview.

When you suspect an interviewer has lured you into a dangerous area, you have three response options.

- **Answer the question.** Realize, however, that you are providing information that is not job-related, and you risk harming your candidacy by responding "incorrectly."

- **Refuse to answer the question.** While you are in your rights to do so, you will probably alienate the employer and come across as uncooperative, confrontational, and hostile. Not exactly the ideal description of a desirable applicant.

- **Reframe the question.** Consider the intent of the question. In other words, try to hear the question behind the question. For example, is the employer asking about your birthplace because there is a concern about your social status, or is it because the interviewer grew up in the same place and is simply trying to make small talk?

Avoid becoming angry, hostile, or argumentative. Calmly examine the clumsily expressed question to uncover the underlying concerns of the interviewer. For example, an employer who questions a woman if she is married or about her plans to have children may not be interested in the candidate's personal life, but rather may be attempting to learn how committed the candidate is to the job. You may answer such a question effectively by saying: *"I am assuming by your question that you are concerned with whether or not I will be able to spend the long hours at the office required to get the work done. I'd like to reassure you by mentioning that throughout school, I held a full time job, did well in my classes, studied long hours in the library and was not held back in any way by any outside responsibilities."* Notice that she has not revealed her plans to have children, yet she has addressed the concerns expressed by the question.

It is appropriate to send a thank you email shortly after an interview. It should be crafted not only to thank people for the time they spent with you and the information that they provided, but also to restate your interest and clarify any pertinent information that you want the employer to remember. Your e-mail should be structured to affirm that you:

- Paid attention to what was said;
- Understood the interviewer's concerns;
- Are excited about the job; that you can and want to do it;
- And, can contribute to the organization immediately.

Some general guidelines for writing strong thank you e-mails include:

- Use correct grammar, good sentence structure and standard business letter format;

- Pinpoint how your abilities, skills and experience relate to the particular needs of the employer as described during the interview. Focus on what you can do for the employer (what credentials, abilities, skills and experience you have that would help the employer), not what the job would do for you;
- Limit your thank-you email to two or three paragraphs;
- And, close by affirming your interest/enthusiasm for the position.

If you interviewed with more than one person, you have two options. You could send a thank you e-mail to each person; however, do not send three or four people the same e-mail. You ought to vary them to reflect a specific aspect of the conversation that you had with each individual. The second option would be to send one to either the most senior person, or the person with whom you established the greatest rapport and "cc" the others.

Try to avoid the temptation of interpreting what the employer is thinking. Just because you do not hear from the employer the next day, or even the next week, do not assume that a rejection will follow. Selecting candidates is a slow, time consuming process. While two weeks on your end of the telephone seems like an eternity, that same timeframe flies by in a flash for an employer. If three or four weeks go by and you have not heard from the employer, call to "check on the status" of your application and reaffirm your interest and enthusiasm for the position. Say:

"I wanted to follow up to see if there is any additional information that I can provide to help you make your decision," or *"I wanted to see if you have any sense of your timeline for making a decision so I can adjust my search accordingly. I am very interested in this opportunity."*

Never bluff and say that you have an offer.

Do yourself — and the employer — a favor: interview as if everything depended on you. Walk in with a clear idea of two or three selling points that you would like to express. Use the interviewer's questions to introduce those points, and back them up with real life examples. At the end of the interview, summarize your qualifications, and articulate your interest and enthusiasm for the job. If you leave the interview having convinced the employer that you have something to offer, nothing — not your color, sex, age, handicap, sexual preference, nationality, etc. — will stand in your way of landing the job that you want. Take as much control of the follow-up process as you can. Be sure to act in a professional manner, project an image of confidence and dependability, and you cannot go wrong.

CHAPTER NINE

STEP 8: EVALUATE AND NEGOTIATE

The interviewing process starts with the employer buying while you sell. But, as you get further along in the process, the balance begins to shift. Once an employer has decided to make an offer to you, that employer is then in a position of selling the job to you. The tone subtly shifts from interviewing to recruiting as the employer is now invested in your candidacy. This creates a more advantageous negotiating position for you. Therefore, the longer you can postpone the salary discussions, the better off you will be.

Some people have unrealistic salary expectations and exaggerated notions of their worth to prospective employers. At the other end of the spectrum are those anxious job seekers who assume that, by putting a low price on their abilities and skills, they will stand a better chance of getting a job offer. If you do not think that you are worth much, neither will an employer. Grounded in your knowledge of the market value of the position, and your ultimate knowledge of your quality, you should develop a preliminary plan. Do not forget to check out www.payscale.com or www.salary.com so that you can have a realistic understanding of what these types of positions pay. You need to be able to articulate what you want *specifically*. Break down your financial and non-pecuniary needs into three categories:

- It would be *great* to have . . .

- I would *like* to have . . .

- I *must* have . . .

To help you focus, review the section on your budget in chapter two, as well as the exercise on *values*. Work through "what if" scenarios. Anticipate compromises and plan exactly how far you are willing to scale back on your needs. When a definite salary offer is made, consider it for several moments before you respond. It is now time to negotiate.

The prospective employer wants to pay a minimum salary to hire a quality employee, which appears to be at odds with your goal of wanting to earn as much as possible. Avoid the trap of viewing negotiating as an adversarial process with winners and losers. Think of it instead as individuals working together to arrive at a mutually beneficial agreement. It is more than trading with others for the things you want, it is discovering ways that you can work together to produce positive results for everyone involved. By using sound business principles, such as preparing and rehearsing, emphasizing accomplishments rather than personal needs, learning and addressing the needs of the employer, asking intelligent questions and listening carefully, your stature is bound to grow, along with your negotiating leverage. Your approach should always be employer-centered, not self-centered. You must be able to describe your worth in relation to the position that has already been defined. Employers do not care that you have been unemployed for seven months; they do not care that you have $80,000 in school loans, or that you have a mortgage, and two children in college. Those facts do not increase your *worth*. What *value* do you bring to the employer? (Review your market research from chapter two.)

Most people hate the thought of negotiating. But the reality is that, if you do not negotiate up front, you may be underpaid by many thousands of dollars over the years. The compensation package that you draw at one organization can set the pattern for the level of income that you can command when negotiating with another employer. Thus, the terms you agree on will have a far reaching impact on your entire career and ultimately, your life. It is not unusual for the difference between the earnings of two individuals to have far less to do with abilities, skills and talents than with each person's ability to negotiate.

A general rule of thumb regarding the discussion of compensation is *never to bring up the subject until an offer of employment has been made*. The goal is to give yourself and the interviewer a chance to get to know one another, so that both of you will have a better idea of how flexible you are willing to be with compensation negotiations. You want to ensure that you acquire enough information about the job, so that you will be able to effectively communicate that you possess the necessary qualifications for the position. Your goal is to get the employer to invest enough time in you so that you can illustrate that you:

- Have done your research on the firm or organization;
- Expect to receive compensation appropriate for your level of qualifications and experience;
- Or, want to be compensated on the basis of performance, not on past salary history.

Understand that before interviewing candidates, employers have established a *predetermined budget* in their minds for the salary that they would like to pay. This figure, of course, is most financially beneficial for the employer. Most employers have some flexibility to negotiate salary, particularly for higher level positions, but, contrary to popular belief, everything is *not* negotiable. Many employers have rigid pay systems — particularly government agencies and corporations that use a lockstep model of compensation. These firms try to keep salaries equitable within the organization by not paying anyone much above the norm. As the interview process progresses, the employer *may* consider altering the budget if impressed by the special skills or background of a particular candidate.

It may be at this point that you are asked what your salary expectations are, but be prepared because the salary question can crop up at any time during the job hunt, and it can come in many forms:

- "What is your current salary?"
- "How much were you paid at your previous employer?"
- "What are your salary requirements?"
- "What is the lowest figure you would accept?"
- "How much do you think you are worth?"
- "Why should we pay you more than other managers?"

You must be prepared to discuss the salary question whenever the *employer* raises the issue. (But remember, *you* should never ask about the salary until you are offered the job.) Be careful. If you state a figure outside of the range the employer has in mind — either too high or too low — you risk having salary used against you as an easy, objective screening device. That is why research during the early stages of your job hunt is so crucial.

Should the salary question arise early in the interview process, and you feel you do not have enough information about the position, try to deflect the question:

- *"I am unclear about the responsibilities of the position. Could you tell me a little more about them?"*
- *"I am looking for a fair market value for the responsibilities involved. I would like to discuss that when I know a little more about what will be required and you know a little more about what I have to offer you."*
- *"My interest is in a complete picture. Salary is just one piece of the puzzle. Professional challenge, growth opportunities,*

benefits, work environment, and relocation are others that will influence my choice. For the right position and company, I am confident that we can come to terms. What about x?" (Redirect the discussion.)

- Or, if said with good-natured humor, you might be effective by asking: *"Are we starting negotiations? Do you have an offer in mind?"* Be careful when using humor. If you use the wrong tone or body language, intended humor could come across as obnoxious.

Another technique you could try is to turn the table:

- "Do you have a range in mind, and, if so, would you mind telling me what that is?"
- "What is the normal range in your organization for a position such as this?"
- "What would the range be for someone with my qualifications?"

By getting the employer to state a range first, you can then place the top of this range into the bottom of yours. For example, if the employer's range is $45,000 - $65,000, your range should be $60,000 - $80,000. Be prepared to articulate why you are worth the salary you are seeking.

If you cannot get the employer to reveal a figure first, try saying:

- "From my research, I learned that the range for marketing directors in this city is __. Does this fit your expectation?" (Or, "Is this the range you were considering?")

Notice this has nothing to do with what you are making now. Rather, it focuses the employers on the requirements of the position and on what a fair market value is for equivalent work. If there is an obvious gap between the ranges and your salary expectations, do not simply end the conversation. Go back to criteria and get off of the subject of salary. Try something like:

"Maybe I didn't understand the requirements of the job. (Restate your understanding of the position.) *Is that a fair description of this position, and are there other requirements? From what you have told me about your needs, I was thinking my skills and background in X and Y* (pick something that emphasizes the unique contributions that you would bring to the job) *would be an asset; do you agree? Also, based on my research, I learned that the range for such a position with your competitors would be..."*

Emphasize the level of skill and talent you bring to the table by citing achievements and using statistics, comparisons, and even testimonials to support your case. In other words, *state your value.* You need to explain why the employer will benefit by paying you more money than the predetermined budget.

Work *with* the employer — not *against* — to arrive at mutually beneficial solutions. Discovering what the other side wants is crucial to arriving at satisfactory agreements. Build a strategy that focuses on working out the best agreement for everyone. Seek to understand all dimensions of an issue. Focusing only on your own immediate payoff can have dire consequences, so learn to consider negotiations from everyone's perspective. Remember, the value of what you have to offer depends on the perceptions of the person or people you are negotiating with. To strengthen your negotiating stance, determine what the employer values and respond accordingly. Ask open-ended questions to learn what is important to the employer. It is your responsibility to calmly educate the employer on the value added component acquired by hiring you.

You can affect — positively or negatively — the way you are positioned in the minds of those with whom you negotiate by the attitude you project. Confidence is an extremely important asset at this phase of the job hunt. Organize your thoughts. Make sure you can get your main point across in the most concise and compelling way. Process an idea through to its logical conclusion by evaluating the possible responses you may get from the other side. Choose your words carefully. Focus on clarity and precision in your speech. State your position firmly. Carry yourself with confidence, and position yourself as a person with negotiating power. In other words, practice, practice, practice.

Be open and honest about what you want, but remember to be careful about how much information that you reveal. Think about what information that you do not necessarily want employers to have. Keep in mind that an interview is not a therapy session. Tell employers what they need to know, or what they ask about. Remember, the more you talk, the more likely you are to sabotage your own efforts — so think through your presentation.

Do not be reticent to ask questions. Skillfully asked questions can transform negotiations from an adversarial conflict into a partnership. By asking questions, you make sure that the employer will talk more and you will talk less. Be careful about the types of questions you ask, and phrase inquiries in positive, neutral terms. Start with open-ended questions, and move on to narrower, more direct questions. Once you have asked a question, be quiet and *listen* to the response.

Throughout the negotiating process, remember to constantly reinforce the perception that you are excited about the offer and that you want to take this position, even if you are disappointed with the figure. You do not want the negotiation to be an argument, but rather a way to get to the place where you want to be in order to accept the offer. Remember, your strategy is to get to your top figure in a way that the employer thinks is fair.

If you are unhappy with what has been offered, it is appropriate to come back with a counter-offer. The key is to emphasize the benefit to the employer of paying you more. Perhaps if the employer cannot meet your salary expectations, you may be able to convince the employer to give you "credit" for additional degrees, superior academic performance, past careers, or skill sets. Perhaps you can convince the employer to create a new position that would better accommodate your skills, interests, and abilities, as well as meeting the employer's needs. If it means moving to a different specialty or industry, keep in mind the employer may want proof of performance *before* feeling justified in giving you the income that you want. Request a review, and increase in six months based on your ability to meet a preset goal. Demonstrate your confidence in your abilities by saying something like:

- "Let me prove I am worth this. I would be happy to come in at this salary if you could agree to review my performance in six months."

Even after you are clear about the offer and are pleased with it, it is in your best interest *not* to accept the job just yet. Take time to reflect on what has been agreed upon:

- *"This sounds terrific. I would like to think it over to make sure we have not missed anything,"* or;

- *"This sounds terrific. I would like to think it over to make sure we have covered everything. What is your timeframe? When would you like my response?"* or;

- "I am very excited about the offer. Can you tell me what your timeframe for a reply is?"

It is common professional courtesy for employers to provide candidates with at least 48 hours to consider an offer.

If you are waiting to hear from other employers, contact them immediately and let them know you have an offer, and would like to clarify your application status before you make any decisions. A second offer in hand could enhance your bargaining power. However, *never* lie about having another offer. While the lie might work, it could backfire and create ill will if the employer finds out. When you compromise your integrity, you demean your value to others, and to yourself.

If you are currently employed, you may find that your current employer is surprised when you announce that you are leaving, and responds with a counter-offer. If you find yourself in this predicament, you may want to ask yourself:

- Why did I interview in the first place? Do I really want to move, or am I happy in my current situation?

- Is this counter-offer an indication of my value to the organization, or simply a stopgap measure to keep me around until they can find a replacement?

- Should I accept the new opportunity, or stay where I have established relationships and a good track record?

Deciding between two offers provokes anxiety. Review your long term goals from chapter one, and consider if either position will enable you to reach your goals more quickly or take you in an entirely different direction. What impact will each position have on other parts of your life?

Exercise 18: Compare and Contrast Offers

To help you make your decision, go back to chapter two and review the values that you identified as "extremely important." List those values and give each one a grade of A to F for how well each position satisfies that value. By comparing the jobs side by side, point-by-point, it will become clear which is better for you.

Extremely Important Values_____ Job 1 _____ Job 2

Be sure to finalize agreements. Do not leave details hanging. It is often amazing how two people sitting in the same room can have quite different perspectives concerning what was agreed upon. To ensure that everyone is clear, you may want to summarize by saying:

> *"So, as I understand it, I will be expected to* (restate your understanding of the position) *in exchange for* (restate the compensation package offered)."

It is important to know when to stop negotiating and start the job. Reaching common ground and setting the stage for mutual respect and cooperation may be more important than the few extra dollars that you might be able to obtain by playing games. Having your priorities in place will help you decide which things you are willing to sacrifice in the negotiating process. Keep the following negotiating tips in mind:

- Find out everything you can before you start to negotiate;
- Design a strategy that focuses on working out the best agreement for everyone;
- Deal fairly and honestly with people;
- Identify one person within the organization to negotiate with;
- Simplify and repeat your message until it sinks in;
- Translate your abilities and skills into benefits for the listener;
- Talk about *value* not *cost;*

- State what you want in clear and concise terms and listen for a response;

- Explore all your options - the more options you can generate, the stronger your position;

- Be prepared to explain why something is unacceptable and offer a counter-solution;

- Finalize all details;

- And, always be mindful about how this negotiation might affect future relations.

Once all the "i"s are dotted and "t"s are crossed, you are ready for your first day at work. Now, the real work begins.

CHAPTER TEN

STEP 9: DEVELOP SOFT SKILLS

As a new employee, it is important to recognize that you are joining an organization with its own set of rules – both written and unspoken – for acceptable behavior. You must learn to be adept at navigating your way through the quagmire of office politics from day one.

Playing office politics conjures up images of the brown-nosing "yes man" willing to sell his soul to get ahead. That is certainly one example; however, that is office politics at its worst. At its best, office politics simply is a cultural assessment of the employer; it is acknowledging how to accomplish things within your organization. Understanding the politics can mean the difference between a mediocre career and a quick rise to stardom. So, whether your goal is to eventually rule the office or simply to get the best assignments, training, experience, and exposure, it is imperative to understand the political landscape.

Just as you needed to learn the job search rules to be effective in your search, now you must understand the rules of your new environment. Knowing the rules will save you from potentially embarrassing, career-altering goofs from which it might be difficult to recover. The written rules will explain things like time off to which you are entitled, reimbursable expenses, perks, and benefits, as well as established procedures for photocopying, proofreading, requesting additional support services, etc. Review Employee Handbooks and other manuals that you received to familiarize yourself with the written rules. This is akin to conducting market research during your job search.

The unspoken or unwritten rules are even more important, though typically less obvious to discern. However, simple observation can uncover the important things. For example, observation can reveal how management reacts to employees who take all the time off to which the written rules say they are entitled; it may reveal that department leaders begin work at 8:00 a.m. each day and *not* 9:00 a.m. as the written policy states. Armed with all this data, you can determine what you need to do to advance your career within the organization.

In addition to knowing the rules, you want to be in the information loop. Listen to rumors and gossip. Do not spread it, do not comment on it, and never believe that it is 100% accurate – but know it. Listen to the gossip to uncover the reputations of your peers and colleagues. Who have been labeled "superstars," "losers," and "troublemakers?" What characteristics do they have in common? Do you share any of these characteristics? Can you emulate the positive characteristics? Can you shed the negative ones? Again, you can learn valuable information through your network. (Aren't you glad you learned those skills during your job search?)

Knowing the reputations of organization leaders will help you uncover not only who the politically powerful players are, but also what skill sets are rewarded in this culture. If your long term goal is to be a leader at this organization, note the common attributes that the leaders possess, and think about ways to begin to develop similar attributes.

Know as much about your organization as possible throughout your tenure there. Periodically review the website, as well as monitor the Facebook page and other literature that your organization distributes to clients and new recruits. These documents shed light on institutional values, cultures, and norms. Remember, information is power.

Speaking of power, it is important to understand it. At every organization, there are two kinds: *Position Power* and *Personal Power*. *Position Power* is based on a person's role within the organization: department manager, committee chair, etc., while *Personal Power* is an individual's innate ability to accomplish tasks and goals no matter where they are in the chain of command. Career advancement is based on your ability to master your personal power. To do so, you must understand the golden rule: people want to work with those they can rely on to do quality work in a timely fashion. By developing a reputation as the "go to" person who happily performs the less desirable assignments with the same level of enthusiasm and attention to detail as the sought after assignments, you will be sought after by the powers that be because you make their lives easier.

With your career on track, time management now becomes the critical skill to master to find the work//life balance that we *all* covet. The ultimate intent of time management is to improve the quality and balance of your life — not simply to speed it up. Time has an elastic quality to it. When you are busy and engaged in what you are doing, there does not seem to be enough of it. When you are bored, it stretches on endlessly. While 24 hours is the same for everyone, it is the *perception* of time that is different. By striving for balance and harmony in all areas of your life, you can alter your current perception of time thereby reducing your stress and increasing your productivity.

Understanding your personal and professional needs is the key to striking the balance between the two. (Review the exercises from chapters one and two.) Successful living is not a matter of success in the workplace *or* at home. It is the product of their combination. Think about how you *really* want to spend your time. With only 168 hours in a week, it is important to analyze how you currently spend it, and how you would reallocate those hours in a "perfect" world. Remember, you only have 24 hours a day to work with.

Exercise 19: Where does the Time Go?

Number of Hours

	Reality	Perfect World
1. Working	_____	_____
2. Commuting	_____	_____
3 Professional development activities (Reading publications, attending Conferences, external meetings, etc.)	_____	_____
4. Paying bills, tending to finances	_____	_____
5. Performing household chores or tasks	_____	_____
6. Participating in family activities	_____	_____
7. Partaking in physical activities	_____	_____
8. Sleeping	_____	_____
9. Pursuing personal interests/hobbies	_____	_____
10. Reading for pleasure	_____	_____
11. Watching TV or Movies	_____	_____
12. Socializing (via phone, e-mail, or events)	_____	_____
13. Attending religious, or spiritual services, praying	_____	_____
14. Volunteering or participating in community life	_____	_____
15. Attending cultural or social events	_____	_____

16. Performing "obligatory" duties _____ _____

17. Other _____ _____ _____

TOTAL **24 hrs** **24 hrs**

CHALLENGE: Jot down 30-50 activities that drain your energy. Divide them into categories (work, home, friends, and/or family). Review your list and determine what choices you could make to minimize or eliminate each drain. Next, list the reasons preventing you from making the choice. Review the Challenges in chapter one to determine how you can move from "I can't because... to How Can I?" How could you modify the choice to eliminate the reason?

Is there is a discrepancy between your "reality" and your "perfect world"? What areas are taking up more of your time than you would like? Are there steps that you can take to make your "perfect world" become your "reality?"

By learning to control your time on a daily level, you are more inclined to be successful at managing the obligations and achieving your overall goals. Follow these tips.

1. Eliminate Clutter.

Things create the illusion of success, but can sometimes create more work. Perhaps your closet is bursting with 500 sweaters that you must plow through daily to find one of the half dozen or so that you actually wear, or your garage is filled with tools that you never use because you can never find them on your workbench. Take a hard look at your things and determine what to keep and what can be tossed.

Paperwork may be the biggest *thing* cluttering your life. When thinking about your personal or professional "paperwork," recognize there is a difference between "data" and "information." Data is the entire universe of facts and statistics on a given topic while information is data that has value to you. It is important to cull through the data and only retain the necessary information. That will eliminate the need to swift through mountains of paper when you need to retrieve information.

Next, put things where you need them. Think in terms of traffic flow. Winter clothes should be in the front of the closet in December and in the back of the closet in July. Active files should be within arms' reach while dormant projects can be filed further away. Also, decide on a filing system or organization structure that plays to your logic track to avoid wasting time looking for needed information or things. Simply having a designated place for everything from your important papers to your keys to your checkbook to the scotch tape and scissors will make your life more manageable.

Like things, relationships can also clutter your life and zap your energy. Identify the toxic relationships in your life. Who are the arsonists, the dramatics, the critics, and the judges? Eliminate those that you can, and develop strategies to minimize the time that you spend with those you cannot eliminate entirely.

2. Think Ahead

The success of every personal and professional project depends on the initial planning stage, so get organized. Start by establishing structures for routine activities to create a semblance of order. That will reduce your stress because you will not have to rethink activities over and over and over again.

No matter the size of the project, for the best results, always start at the end and work backwards. Consider the deadline, estimate the length of time that each task will take, consider if several tasks can be completed simultaneously, and examine the resources that you *have* versus the resources you *need* to make contingency plans to get the job done despite any obstacles. Consider related issues that may impact the success of your project (e.g. conference room availability or other anticipated demands on your time). Finally, always ask yourself *"who else needs to know?"* to make sure your project does not adversely impact the work or lives of others.

It is often said, *"the devil is in the details."* The only way to stay ahead of the devil is to invest the time to think through the details of each project. Depending on the complexity of each project, this critical step could take five minutes or five hours. Either way, the time invested in the beginning of the project is likely to pay off tenfold in time saved over the life of the project. (Can you see the parallel between self-assessment before launching a job search and strategizing before launching a project? Same skill set, different application).

3. Prioritize

Because you have planned and organized, you can map out the sequence of the various tasks that need to be accomplished with the help of To-Do Lists and Calendars. Charting everything that needs to be done enables you to prioritize and maximize effectiveness.

Start with the biggest task that will take the longest time to complete. Once the project is underway, you can use any "wait" time to:

- Work on other, smaller projects;
- Respond to emails;
- Return phone calls;
- Tend to administrative tasks;
- Catch up on professional reading or
- Or, tend to quick personal tasks.

The key error that most people make is to focus solely on the immediate task at hand. Such an approach causes us to operate constantly in reactive mode. By opting to think through the longer term projects first and getting them underway (particularly if they involve other people), you will be able to identify the smaller tasks to fill in any downtime, thereby using your time more efficiently. Whenever possible, adopt a "*do it now*" mentality. Most stress comes from that nagging sensation that we forgot to do something, or from looking for lost items. By handling matters as they arise (add them to your To Do List immediately), you can eliminate such stress and use your time more productively.

We all have parts of the day when we operate at a higher level. Note when your brain surge is and save complex projects for that time. Also, develop defense strategies to mitigate any weaknesses. That will prevent you from procrastinating because you will know how to tackle those difficult projects.

4. Manage Technology

Some people view technology as a blessing; others, a curse. If you respond to every telephone ring, e-mail buzz, and blackberry vibration like Pavlov's dog responded to the bell, you likely fall into the latter category. But technology truly can make your life easier, if you learn to manage it well. For example, when you are working on a project requiring intense concentration, work in 45 minute spurts. Use the other 15 minutes to check voicemail or e-mails. Respond to the critical issues during that time and the others at a designated time later in the day. This method will ensure that no one ever needs to wait more than an hour to get a response to a critical issue and that each message will have your full and undivided attention. *Listen or read the entire message and provide complete and detailed responses.* There is nothing that wastes more time than the volley of half-answered emails lobbed back and forth every day in the workplace and at home. Slow down, be accurate, save time.

Finally, live by the 24-hour rule. Respond to every voicemail or e-mail within 24 hours. Even if your response is simply *"I will have the information for you next week,"* do not wait until next week to respond. Otherwise, you will have to waste time responding to e-mails or voicemails asking *"did you get my message?"*

Effective communication is perhaps the most important "soft" skill to master. Not only is it the greatest time saving device, effect communication is critical in every aspect of your professional life — from networking and interviewing, to supervising and delegating, to working with clients, peers, and superiors. It is also a basic life skill that can be used to enhance your personal life. While you cannot control how other people share or process information, you can consider their style and adapt your own style to improve communication.

The purpose of adjusting your style to others is not simply to be nice. It is more self-serving than that. By giving your listeners what *they* need, you are more likely to get what *you* need from the exchange.

For example, is your listener a fast-moving, action-oriented extrovert, or a quiet, thoughtful introvert? Is this someone who likes detail and information, or only bottom-line information? Is this someone with whom you can think out loud or someone who only wants to hear the end decision? By being mindful of your own behavioral tendencies, you can improve your communication skills, and, ultimately, your likeability.

Do not discount the importance of likeability in the workplace. Strong communicators have a distinct advantage in the world because they know how to relate to people and get things done.

People are judged not only by the words that they choose to articulate a thought, but also by the tone and body language used during the delivery. It is important to be mindful of the images that you project. You want to ensure that any inferences made about you accurately reflect who you are, and the intent of your message. This is not to suggest that form is more important than substance. However, you never want your "form" to impede your ability to effectively relay your message. Reread page 97 to refresh your memory of the best way to leverage your nonverbal assets.

Effective communicators know how to work with others, and have mastered the art of delegation. Delegating is an often overlooked, yet essential skill to master as you advance in your career. Its purpose is to enable you to dispose of simpler tasks to free you up to perform tasks which are of greater *value* to you personally or your organization. The time that it takes up front to orchestrate a plan of action, explain the desired outcome, and monitor the progress of each staff (or family) member ultimately requires less time than it would take to execute the entire action plan yourself. That is, if you delegate *correctly.*

You are hampering your ability to delegate effectively if you:

- Believe can do the task better or faster yourself;
- Worry that a subordinate might not do the task properly and, because you are ultimately accountable, your professional reputation may be at risk;
- And, fear that if the subordinate does do it well, you may be viewed as "non-essential" or expendable.

The truth is that you probably *can* do the specific task better and faster. However, as you move up the hierarchy, additional responsibilities will also require your attention at work, and at home. With the same amount of hours in each day and multiplying responsibilities, you have to use every available resource to get all the work done. Accept the fact that, occasionally, it will take more time to explain to someone else how to do something than it would take to do it yourself. Delegate it anyway. The next time, it will take less time to explain. More importantly, you will be developing your team (and family) for the future and, thus, ultimately gain the desired leverage and control you are seeking. And remember, people rise or fall to the level of expectation. Delegate tasks and hold people accountable. The better your team does under your leadership, the more *value* you will bring to your organization. No one has ever lost a job for being too productive.

Remember: *"the success of every project depends on the initial planning stage."* Invest the time at the beginning of the project to think through the project to its conclusion. This will enable you to clearly define the goals and objectives, assign the tasks, and assess the progress to ensure that you get the end result you want. You must develop a strategy to deal with any potential problems *before* they arise.

Imagine that you are managing a project with a definitive deadline. Distracted by other obligations and responsibilities, you do not invest the time to think through the project to its conclusion. As a result, you do not consider how long the main task will take. The ancillary tasks you completed earlier become outmoded and need to be updated, creating more work and more stress. You are forced to race through a task that ideally requires more time and attention, and then something you completely forgot sends you scrambling and working late into the night. The people involved are crabby and stressed. The job gets done, but the cost is high.

- To avoid such nightmare scenarios, at the start of each project consider:
- What is the goal or desired end result?
- What is the deadline for the project?
- Can some of the tasks be carried out in parallel?
- Are there competing projects within the department or institution with higher priorities that are going to take up key resources?
- How many people are *needed* to accomplish the goal? How many people are *available* to work on the project? What type of skills do they need to possess?

Once you know who is on the team, and have a sense of their strengths and weaknesses, you will want to decide what level of delegation is appropriate for their skill level and your comfort level.

As you work more and more with people and trust develops, you will get more comfortable delegating at higher levels. Treat delegating as a chance to build rapport. Chat with subordinates about what needs to get done, how they intend to do it, and why it is important. Investing 10 minutes in the process takes extra effort up front, but there is sure to be timesaving payoff.

Always operate under the principal that you can never be too clear. As the delegator, it is your responsibility to ensure your team knows:

- **Goals and Objectives of the project.** Too many busy professionals delegate under the command and control style of "do this because I said so." They believe that it will take too long to explain the details. However, if everybody understands the overall objective (which typically can be explained in three sentences in less than 30 seconds) or how their segment of the project ties into the overall goal or impacts other aspects of the project, they will be more cooperative.)

- **Operating Procedures.** Confirm how information will be shared (e-mail, voicemail, meetings, etc.), who else is working on the project, and any other peculiarities specific to this project.

- **SPECIFIC Deadlines.** *"ASAP"* is meaningless. So is *"in a few days."* Try, *"I need it in an hour"* or *"I need it Wednesday afternoon."* Leave no room for ambiguity. Setting specific deadlines and allowing your team to manage their own workload will ameliorate your constant need to hover and inquire *"Is it done yet?"* to the relief of both you and your team members.

- **Expected performance standards.** Even if you believe people should know what is expected of them — take the 10 seconds required to state the obvious. You can never be too clear.

- **How they are doing along the way.** When appropriate, provide on-going feedback to allow for corrections to be made as the project progresses.

The other side of delegating is delivering meaningful feedback. Most people hate the thought of giving feedback. Not only is it time consuming, it can be emotionally draining. What if the listener cries, gets defensive, or threatens to sue? Perhaps the feedback will fall on deaf ears. Why bother?

We bother because the cost of *not* sharing feedback outweighs those obstacles. If people are not told that they have done something incorrectly they will continue to repeat the behaviors, and you will continue to be frustrated. At work, productivity will drop, people will likely lose their jobs and the company will lose talent and money. At home, tensions will rise.

To avoid such needless human and financial costs, learn to deliver meaningful feedback informally and continuously. Think beyond annual performance appraisals. Meaningful on-going informal feedback enhances the formal process because staff members will have received messages throughout the year offering immediate corrective action for very specific behaviors in a timely manner. The formal review can then be used to reinforce those message and focus on systematic goal setting to ensure that the professional development of each staff member for the benefit of the organization. Effective feedback:

- Creates *trust* and *cooperation;* it focuses on *improvements,* both possible and those actually achieved.
- *Increases* skills.
- *Improves* confidence in ability and potential.
- *Clarifies* exactly where people stand and what to do next.

- Leaves people feeling *helped and empowered.*
- When delivered properly, not only will effective feedback eliminate undesirable behaviors, it will also increase skills and performance and create an atmosphere of trust and cooperation.

Use the CORRECT format to deliver informal feedback effectively.

C - Caption/Headline

"Let us talk about the XYZ project you worked on last week."

O - Observed behaviors

"I noticed you did…" Explain what specific actions lead to the error. *"You screwed up"* is not useful. Try instead, *"you researched issue X when I asked you to focus on issue Y."*

R - Rx

Explain the proper "prescription" or process that should have been used. *"You should have done…"*

R - Request explanation

It is important to calmly ask questions to uncover why the person did what she did. Maybe she was just careless, but maybe she uncovered other information that could be vital. Ask, *"is there a reason you did it the way you did?"* (The reason might be valid.)

E - Explain preferred behavior

Give the person the opportunity to figure out alternative ways to correct the problem. Ask, *"how might you have handled that differently?"* See if they can identify the option. If not, say, *"In the future you should do…"* (Repeat the Rx.)

C - Confirm understanding

"Do you understand?" Or *"do you have any questions?"*

T - Take action

(Monitor to ensure behavior changes.)

These time management, communication, delegating, and feedback skills are applicable in the home as well as the workplace. Many hands make light work. People want to help. (In the workplace, they are *paid* to help.) Let them. Whether you enlist spouses, children, or retired parents to assist with household chores or hire housekeepers, handymen, etc. to lighten your load, delegate effectively and provide meaningful feedback to reduce stress and create harmony.

There is no magic pill to achieve life/work balance. There will always be factors beyond your control that demand your time and attention. Yet, with a keen understanding of your own strengths and weaknesses, wants and needs, as well as careful planning, you can minimize the amount of time spend in "reactive" mode and reduce the amount of stress in your personal and professional life.

Organize and develop systems to create a semblance of order. Learn to delegate, provide on-going meaningful feedback, and communicate directly at work and at home to reduce the hours of wasted time. And remember, anything and everything is possible if you have the mind set and attitudes that support your success.

CHAPTER ELEVEN

STEP 10: CULTIVATE YOUR BRAND

In chapter two, you learned that self-knowledge is the most reliable tool to run an effective job search and ensure career success. The ABCs apply throughout your career. You must continually:

- catalogue your *ABILITIES;*
- acknowledge your *BELIEFS;*
- *COMMUNICATE* your message effectively.

Maintain your own personnel file that contains information about your long term and short term goals, as well as significant assignments and accomplishments, seminars attended, professional and community activities, etc. Think of it as an unedited resume. Update this document quarterly. Use this information to prepare an "annual report" prior to your annual performance appraisal. Even if your employer does not deliver performance appraisals, carve out time each year to pause, reflect, and take stock.

Exercise 20: Take Stock

Each year, *before* your formal evaluation, take stock of your own performance. List:

- Major projects worked on;
- Significant accomplishments for the past year;
- List any knowledge, skills, or abilities not being fully utilized in my assignments; describe how they might be used better;

- List internal activities you participated in that contribute to the organization's mission (i.e., recruiting, committee assignments, etc);

- And, list professional and community activities of the last twelve months. Include external activities (speaking engagements, articles written, conventions and seminars attended, community activities, etc.).

Ask:

1. Is my workload insufficient, satisfactory, or too much?

2. Am I receiving a sufficient variety of assignments to enable me to grow? If not, what can I do to address the issue?

3. Have I had regular opportunities to discuss my work with supervisors? If not, what could I have done differently to get needed feedback?

4. Have I received and acted on supervisors' suggestions for improving my work?

5. What are my goals for the next year? In what areas would I like to improve and what is my action plan to accomplish this?

Remember, no one cares more about your career development than you do. Take the lead and avail yourself of every resource available to you, including professional relationships. You should be concerned with the process of building and using networks as a permanent aspect of your career to broaden your field of vision in order to make informed, smart decisions. It is imperative to establish strong mentor relationships from the start of your career. Who you know is important, but who knows you is the key to solidifying your professional brand. The networking skills you perfected in chapter five are equally applicable in this context.

Participate in formalized mentor programs; however, do not rely solely on such programs, or simply hope people will notice you and offer to take you under their wings. It is not enough. Solid mentor relationships evolve naturally, not through administration. Certainly participate in formal programs, but do more. Create a support system, or a Board of Advisors. Establishing a network of mentors will allow you to learn from different styles, develop a range of skills, and consider various perspectives of an issue. Think of these people as resources to help you develop your brand, plan and execute your career goals, and help you navigate difficult situations.

Network internally to increase the chances of making an impression on decision makers, monitor the rumor mill, and learn about business groups beyond your own. Volunteer for committee assignments; attend corporate events; simply strive to be visible in the organization and build a reputation as a good corporate citizen.

Remember: *Self-Assessment + Market Assessment = Career Success.* Today's world is changing constantly. Be mindful of economic forces and world events that will impact your career journey. It is important to be up-to-date about changes impacting your industry. Pay attention to your environment and use your pre-established goals to map out a path to avoid any obstacles, while at the same time developing strategies to cope with inevitable transitions.

Consider any difficulties (personal or professional) that may have impeded your performance, but do not put this information in writing. Think about whether or not it would be appropriate to verbally share that information with your employer. For example, if tending to a family illness earlier in the year is responsible for lower than expected performance, it might be helpful to point that out so your productivity can be viewed in perspective. Carefully consider the information that you want to share. And, even if you choose not to share specific information, if there is something impacting your performance, make sure that you design a strategy to deal with it before it becomes a bigger issue.

Benchmark your progress against your colleagues. If others appear to be getting more sophisticated work, ask yourself why. Is it because you have not proven yourself to be reliable? Is your substantive work not up to par? Perhaps you have not mastered the needed time management, communication, delegation, or feedback skills required for the role. Answers to these questions can help you see yourself through the eyes of your superiors and enable you to address issues before they become monumental. And, before you assume that there is some great conspiracy by the power structure to sabotage your career, determine how your behavior may be contributing to the situation and try to correct that first.

Transitions typically fall into one of four categories:

- **Anticipated and voluntary**. In a perfect world, all transitions would be the result of strategic decisions initiated by you.

- **Unanticipated and voluntary**. Sometimes, through no direct action on your part, the perfect opportunity lands in your lap. You have the luxury of accepting or declining the opportunity based on your current needs and interests.

- **Anticipated but involuntary**. Many times, people wait until others make a career decision for them. There may be warning signs that a transition is imminent, but rather than take action, you wait, allowing others to control your fate.

- **Unanticipated and involuntary.** Perhaps the most unsettling transitions fall into this category; typically, they tend to be negative. Everything was going along as usual — or so you thought. You believed that you were productive; you know that you have been busy. Your last reviews were positive, and you even received a year-end bonus. You did not see any warning signs until the transition was thrust upon you. They can also occur as the result of some unexpected, life-altering event like an illness, death of a loved one, or world event. Sometimes, life happens and disrupts our plans.

To avoid experiencing involuntary transitions at work, pay close attention, and constantly assess and reassess your current situation. Look for clues like:

- Having difficulty with a supervisor;
- Being assigned less important tasks/duties;
- Not receiving bonus;
- Being avoided by supervisors, colleagues, subordinates;
- Receiving negative feedback/performance review;
- Not being personally productive or engaged in your job;
- Or, changes in the economy or business cycle that might impact your industry.

If you see these signs, take action. Either fix the problem (if possible), or recognize that you cannot change the situation (and sometimes you cannot through no fault of your own) and strategize your next move. Always try to avoid unanticipated and involuntary situations by actively anticipating and constructing self-directed voluntary transition plans.

One of the greatest impediments to change in any undertaking is that people withdraw from a situation rather than explore what the alternatives might be. It is possible to find joy in your work. Successful alternative arrangements *are* possible – *if* you are willing to diverge from the norm. Trust yourself, others, and the process to lead you to a better way. Once you have evidence of the possibilities, it will be easier to take action.

Understand that the way that you think about a transition can make it easy to handle or impossible to manage. It is not the event that is determinative; rather, it is the way you choose to experience the event. Believe that you have choices. Believe that you can create your own possibilities. Do not allow "should" to force you down a path that you do not want to go. Your only limitation is imposed by the NAILs that keep you stuck (refer back to chapter two) and they reside in your imagination.

Your frame of mind affects your actions. For example:

Bad Attitude

- I screwed up. I will never work again.
- There is no more bankruptcy work. I do not know how to do anything else.
- The real estate market has dried up here. I will be living in my car soon.

Improved Attitude

- It was a hard lesson to learn, but I will be better having learned it.
- I will use what I know about bankruptcy to segue into debt financing work.
- I will relocate to where the real estate market is hot.

Attitude drives behavior, and a positive attitude is critical to success. This is especially true in the case of involuntary transitions. They are the most traumatic because they imply "failure." Even when you know it is time to leave your position, your ego takes a pounding when someone else tells you that it is time to move on. But consider the following failures:

- **Babe Ruth** struck out 1330 times in route to the Hall of Fame.
- **Elvis Presley** was banished from the Grand Ole Opry after only one performance and told, "you ain't going nowhere, son."
- **Oprah Winfrey** was fired from her job as a TV reporter and advised, "you're not fit for TV."
- **Walt Disney**'s first cartoon production company went bankrupt.

- **John Grisham**'s first novel, *A Time to Kill*, was rejected by 15 agents and a dozen publishing houses.
- **Edgar Allan Poe** was expelled from West Point.
- **Abraham Lincoln** lost eight elections, failed at two businesses, and had a nervous breakdown before becoming our 16th President.

Nothing succeeds like failure. Learning opportunities, which are necessary for growth and development, sometimes come in the form of what would traditionally be defined as "failure." The world is filled with examples of people who used failure as a springboard to success. This is not to suggest that you should go out of your way to fail in order to achieve your career goals. Simply accept the fact that failures are going to happen. Readjust the prism through which you view such failures, and you can use them to your advantage.

The important thing is that you take charge of your own career / life development. Identify the changes that you need or want to make, and then be proactive about making those changes happen. *Assume responsibility.* No one cares about your career/life development more than you do. Do not wait for others to lead you through the quagmire. Remember, planning your career is like solving a business problem. Define objectives, develop strategies, monitor progress, and take corrective action when needed. The beauty of the career/life planning process is that *you* get to define the objectives based on your life rules and personal definition of success.

If you determine a course correction is warranted, do something about it. Rather than stay on an unfulfilling path because it is what you know, take action. It is scary to head into the unknown. But, remember that basic principle you learned in high school physics: *bodies in motion stay in motion; bodies at rest stay at rest.* Be bold; take action. However you choose to proceed, know that as long as you are able to demonstrate to employers that there is a well thought out, coherent plan aimed at building a portfolio of skills, the choice will be well received.

Think about the direction you'd like your life to take. Go back to chapter two and review the *Perfect Job Challenge*. Determine what type of experiences you need, or what types of decisions that you need to make, in order to progress along your preferred path. Stretch yourself to acquire new skills and knowledge to remain in constant demand, and at the same time invest in developing an expertise. Such a strategy will enable you to have a competitive advantage. Specializing in one area alone can be risky, market pressures may render you obsolete. Simply make sure that you are not so much of a generalist that you have not developed proficiency in any particular skill. A balance of the two is a better strategy. Base your mix of expertise and flexibility on the overall development goal that you set. Areas of new exposure are not limited to the development of technical expertise, but include other more general skills as well. As you develop your technical skills, don't forget to focus on "soft" skills — things like working in teams, time management, negotiating, communicating, understanding diversity, delegating, and adapting to change. Such intangibles are often "silent discriminators," indicating who is on the fast track and who is not. Soft skills enable you to apply your hard skills in a variety of situations, thereby increasing your value to the employer. By serving as an officer or director of community groups, on alumni boards, or in church and synagogue groups, you can build these skills. Experience gained in any situation counts.

You may determine that you are on the correct path. In that instance, your action plan would simply be to continue doing what you have been doing and reevaluate your progress annually to compare your achievements to your intended objectives. Each year, ask yourself:

- Am I satisfied with my current career or life situation?
- Has any new exposure sought been gained?

- Has my level of responsibility increased? Is that what I want?
- Does the current work environment continue to be receptive to my career objectives?

When the answer to these questions is no, you may determine that a change in employment, a redirection of your career path, or an industry shift is in order. Think about the choices that you have made. Can you make a different choice to realign your career with your goals? Revisit the reflections exercise that you completed in chapter two.

As you travel towards your dream, you want to position yourself to always be in the proper mental and financial state to take advantage of opportunities as they arise. Any change at work will impact your life, *and* any change in your life may very well impact your work too. For example, embarking on a new job or career when you are in the middle of an unsettling divorce, tending to a terminally ill family member, or starting a family may not be a good idea. Do what you can to manage such events to limit their impact on your career choices, but accept that some things are simply beyond your control.

While you cannot always control your emotional state, you can typically control your financial situation. Tend to your finances early in your career. Managing your finances from the beginning of your career will provide you with the freedom to pursue opportunities of interest throughout your career. Financial security creates an air of confidence and independence, and allows you to follow your passions and live well. Refer back to the exercise in chapter two to revise your budget.

Do not hesitate to spend some of your own money to ensure your employability. Invest in training, career development, and education. Enroll in seminars and workshops covering topics like public speaking, management, or client development to enhance your portfolio of abilities and skills. Consider periodically consulting with a career coach to keep you focused and on track.

Make wise choices about which investments to make. Education and training alone do not ensure success, as many well-educated, unemployed professionals can tell you. For example, while an advanced degree *may* increase your marketability in some of the more technical fields or help you transition from one specialty to another by providing intense training and knowledge quickly, an advanced degree could also *decrease* your marketability. Some employers have their own training programs and hesitate to hire candidates with advanced degrees who command higher salaries. Before you decide to invest in any educational program, make sure you are doing it because you have a genuine interest in the subject matter, not simply to add a credential to your resume. Find out if your employer (or target employer) values the extra schooling and do a cost to benefit analysis. Remember not only to factor in tuition and related school costs, but also your lost wages during the time you are in graduate school.

Whether you find yourself in a transition voluntarily or involuntarily, you will no doubt ask yourself questions like:

- Is there some way to combine my work with my other equally important interests?

- Are there jobs available at my level and salary expectations, or will I have to settle for less?

- Do I give up on my chosen field and do something else, and if so, what else can I do?

These questions can be overwhelming because there are no immediate answers. Do not get stymied and opt to stay stuck in an unhappy situation, or simply avoid the questions altogether. Playing it safe and staying in a position that you have outgrown will damage your career. Remember, choosing to do nothing is still a choice that you are making. Most people end up happier after a transition. The hard part is living through the unavoidable discomfort and uncertainties.

How often you change positions, jobs, or careers typically matters less than *why*. However, you must be able to articulate a logical progression down a coherent path. Do you have a good story line? Employers easily understand people moving on to develop new skills or industry knowledge, or to broaden their portfolio of experiences. However, when the moves appear to be a chase for salary increases or fancy titles only, your loyalty, and perhaps judgment, may be questioned. The onus is on you to articulate the story line and illustrate the wisdom in the decisions that you have made along the way. Again, refer back to the *Reflect* exercise completed in chapter two to help you create your story line.

As you can see, we end where we began. Career success is a circular and continuous process that requires you to continually assess and articulate the value that you add to the marketplace based on your abilities and interests. That involves a dedication to continuous learning and regularly benchmarking your abilities and skills, nurturing your professional relationships and monitoring changes in the workplace. Remember:

Self-Assessment + Market-Assessment = Career Success!

It also requires maintaining a future focus to anticipate and plan for transitions. A focused, but flexible, career development plan will serve you well throughout your work life. As the Dalai Lama once said, *"happiness is not something ready-made… It comes from your own actions."*

You have the power to create the career — and life — you want, but you have to *do* something to make it happen. Take action and enjoy the journey.

APPENDIX

WEB RESOURCES

Consider this a preliminary list of websites to launch your job search. To help you assess which websites are the best ones to use to meet your specific objectives, consider:

- the number and kinds of jobs posted on the site;
- the primary salary levels of the posted jobs;
- the cost of using the site;
- how easy the site is to navigate, how well it is maintained and how often it is updated.

If you choose to post your resume in a searchable database, make sure there is a confidentiality feature so that your contact information will not be distributed until you agree to release it to a specific employer. Also, make sure those resumes are dated so you can confirm a resume is the most current version.

Finally, if you do not see what you are looking for here, google "jobs in (industry) or (geography)" to find additional useful sites. Remember to save the ones you like under favorites.

GENERAL JOB BOARDS (FREE)

https://georgian-csm.symplicity.com/
http://www.careerbuilder.com/
http://www.monster.com
http://www.glassdoor.com/
http://www.snagajob.com/
http://www.simplyhired.com/
http://www.internships.com/
http://www.indeed.com
http://www.simplyhired.com
http;//www.ziprecruiter.com
http://www.snagajob.com/
http://www.internships.com/

FEE BASED JOB BOARDS

https://www.theladders.com/
http://www.policyjobs.net
http://www.politicaljobs.net
http://www.hound.com/

ACADEMIC JOBS

http://jobs.chronicle.com/section/Jobs/61/
http://www.academickeys.com/all/choose_discipline.
php?go=find_a_job
http://www.academic360.com/

BLUE COLLAR JOBS

http://www.bluecollarjobs.com/
http://www.unionjobs.com

COMMUNICATIONS/MEDIA

http://www.iwantmedia.com/jobs/

ENGINEERING JOBS

http://www.engineerjobs.com/

http://www.engcen.com/engineering.asp

ENVIRONMENTAL JOBS

www.ehscareers.com

www.Ecojobs.com

www.Environmentaljobs.com

www.ejobs.org

www.sustainablebusiness.com/jobs

www.ecoemploy.com/jobs

FINANCE JOBS

www.efinancialcareers.com

www.jobsearchdigest.com

http://www.careers-in-finance.com/re.htm

GOVERNMENT JOBS

http://www.justice.gov/careers/careers.html

http://www.usajobs.gov/

http://www.opm.gov/job_seekers/

http://plum.jobs.topusajobs.com/

http://thehill.com/employment/

http://hillzoo.com (select employment)

http://www.senate.gov/employment/po/positions.htm

http://www.uscourts.gov

HOSPITALITY JOBS

http://www.hcareers.com/

http://www.hospitalityonline.com/

http://www.hospitalityjobsite.com/

http://wineandhospitalityjobs.com/

INTERNATIONAL JOBS

http://www.internationaljobs.org/

http://www.fpa.org

LEGAL JOBS

http://www.cable360.net/jobs.html

http://jobs.law360.com/

www.lawcrossings.com

www.gobiglaw.com

www.goinhouse.com

MEDICAL JOBS

http://www.medicaljobs.org/

http://www.healthecareers.com/

http://www.allhealthcarejobs.com/

PHILANTHROPY/NON-PROFIT JOBS

http://philanthropy.com/section/Jobs/224/

http://www.humanrightsjobs.com/

http://www.idealist.org/

http://www.psjd.org/

http://foundationcenter.org/getstarted/guides/job.html

http://www.rileyguide.com/nonprof.html#think

http://www.rileyguide.com/jobs.html#law

http://www.policyjobs.net/

PUBLIC RELATIONS JOBS

http://www.prsa.org/jobcenter/

SPORTS JOBS

www.jobsinsports.com

http://www.teamworkonline.com/

TECHNOLOGY JOBS

http://www.dice.com/

WRITING/PUBLISHING JOBS

http://www.writejobs.com/

http://www.bookjobs.com/

http://www.mediabistro.com/Magazine-Publishing-jobs.html

RESEARCH TOOLS

http://www.bls.gov/ooh/occupation-finder.htm

http://www.payscale.com/

http://www.salary.com/

http://money.cnn.com/magazines/fortune/bestcompanies/

http://www.forbes.com/pictures/efkk45fmmj/the-top-hiring-
    companies-in-15-big-cities/

http://www.highlandsco.com

ABOUT THE AUTHOR

Kathleen Brady, CPC is a career/life management coach, author, and motivational speaker with 25 years of experience helping people identify and integrate their personal and professional goals. She inspires clients to embrace their dreams and offers practical action steps to bring them to life. Kathleen shows her clients how to develop a comprehensive career/life strategy to achieve career success and live happy and joyful lives.

A sought-after industry speaker, Brady is known for her directness and humor. She is a recognized expert on topics including job search strategies, and career/life success skills such as goal setting, communication, leadership, time management, and stress reduction. A frequent contributor to *Your Money* in the New York Daily News, she also has shared her expertise on **Fox News, CNN, NPR,** *This Week in America, First Business Report,* and radio stations across the country, offering advice on how to enjoy success at work and at home.

Brady is currently Director of Career Services and Adjunct Instructor at **Georgian Court University**, principal of **Brady & Associates CareerPlanners, LLC,** a career/life management company, and **Kanarek & Brady**, a career transition company specializing in the legal profession. She started her career at **Columbia Law School,** and went on to serve as Assistant Dean of Career Services at **Fordham University School of Law**, National Director of Staff Recruitment and Development at **Jackson Lewis,** and Manager of Associate Professional Development at **Milbank Tweed Hadley & McCloy, LLP**. She is also a past President of the **National Association for Law Placement,** and a founding member of the **NALP Foundation for Research and Education.** She has published countless articles and three books: *GET A JOB! 10 Steps to Career Success* (Inkwater Press, 2013); *Navigating Detours on the Road to Success: A Lawyer's Guide to Career Management* (Inkwater Press, 2005); and, *Jobs for Lawyers, Effective Techniques for Getting Hired in Today's Legal Marketplace* (Impact Publications, 1996). She is a **Certified Professional Coach**, a **Master Practitioner** of the Energy Leadership Index, a certified provider of the Highlands Ability Battery, and a member of the **International Coach Federation and the American Society of Journalists and Authors.**

Kathleen lives on the Jersey Shore with her husband John Currie.

CPSIA information can be obtained at www.ICGtesting.com
Printed in the USA
BVOW11s0116070815

411914BV00005B/10/P